A LIFE ON THE LINE

Stories of Service in the Border Patrol

1970s – 1990s

By

Darryl Rambo

Paperback ISBN 978-1-60145-568-0
Hardcover ISBN 978-1-60145-579-6

Printed in the United States of America.

Booklocker.com, Inc.
2008

Dedication

I am dedicating this book to the two most important people in my life.

Jackie, my wife and mother of our four children, was there by my side throughout this entire story. This dedication is in her memory as she lost her ten year battle with cancer in 1993, two years prior to my retirement.

Lily and I have been married now for 13 years. Without her this story would not be in print today. She has been, and is still my biggest supporter. For that I thank her.

CONTENTS

Forward

I served twenty three years with the U.S. Government; two of those years were in the U.S. Army, twenty one were served with the Border Patrol, of those with the Border Patrol ten years were served in El Paso, Texas. This book covers those ten years in El Paso.

There were many humorous, strange, odd, and sometimes just plain malicious things that happened during my career. This book contains some of those events.

I have tried in this book to humanize the Border Patrol. For too many years the Border Patrol has been the invisible agency. People hear about them, but hardly anyone ever sees them. Since 9/11 the public is hearing more, and more about the Border Patrol, but is what they are hearing true? Was the Border Patrol responsible for 9/11? They absolutely were not.

Throughout the years prior to 9/11 the U.S. Border Patrol Central Office consisted of one little rag tag office in Washington D.C. This is how serious the United States Government took the United States Border Patrol.

Although most of the contents of this book happened a few years ago, nothing has changed; it's all timeless Border Patrol. Twenty years ago when I caught groups of people from countries other than Mexico, and there was no room for them at the detention center, or in the city, or county jail, I would have to write them up on a form I-210 (Order to Show Cause), and turn them loose on their own recognizance. They were supposed to appear before a judge within 30 days, but they never did. They now had this sheet of paper that allowed them to go anywhere in the United States, and just disappear, which they did, and still do to this day. Even after September 11, 2001 this is still the practice. One of the reasons for writing this book is to make U.S. Citizens aware that this is happening, and hopefully, one day something will be done about it.

This shortage of detention facilities is not the fault of the Border Patrol. It is the fault of the United States Government. They are fully aware of these aliens being turned loose and they are doing nothing about it. In fact they are the reason for them being turned loose. We need housing to detain aliens even more than we need additional agents.

CHAPTER 1

Out of the Woods

Just a short stop at Hingham, Montana to pick up my sister Gaynelle and sister-in-law Twyla, but I will have to make up that time if I'm going to arrive in Lincoln, Montana on schedule. I will save at least thirty minutes time by taking the Rudyard cut-off, and when you're in the trucking business time is everything. It's a good road as long as the weather is good, and as far as I can see the weather looks good. Of course it is dark, so I can't really see that well. The first fifteen miles of the cut-off is paved, but the other two-thirds have a gumbo base that can be as slick as snot when it's wet. Nothing for us to worry about though; at sundown the sky looked completely clear.

We're on the gumbo, rolling along real smooth, a big cloud of dust billowing out behind us. Then all of a sudden, without warning its raining and we're in the mud. Trying to drive that 18-wheeler on slippery gumbo is like trying to stuff a wet noodle up a wildcat's ass. I manage to keep it in the middle of the road until it coasts to a stop. We sit there perfectly still for about five seconds, maybe ten; then the back-end of the trailer very slowly begins to slide off the road on the passenger's side. I watch in the rear-view mirrors, completely fascinated. As the trailer wheels slide down into the ditch, I watch with curiosity as the trailer frame twists, I'm wondering if it will just keep on flexing or if it will break free like it's supposed to or if it will flip us over. Sponggg! Just like that, there's the answer.

I'm thrown against the top of the cab, and then I drop down on top of Ray, my relief driver. Gaynelle and Twyla, and all their baggage are piled up at the passenger side of the sleeper, which is now the bottom of the sleeper. I ask if they are all right, and they tell me they are. I'm the only one to get hurt. I'm not sure how much I'm hurt, but judging by the amount of blood I'm losing; my throat must have been cut. The girls have a look at it and determine that I'm bleeding from a small cut on my ear lobe. I also have some broken ribs that hurt like hell. The rain continues.

It's my truck, and I am driving, so I feel it's my responsibility to go for help. There's a farmhouse about a mile or a mile and a half across the plowed fields, and it looks like that's going to be the nearest help. I head off in that direction walking through the mud. This isn't going to be easy, but it will give me some time to think about my future. I never expected to be a trucking tycoon, now there isn't any doubt. I'm going to lose my truck, that's for sure. There doesn't appear to be that much damage to the truck, but I can't make that twelve hundred dollar a month payment without a truck, and I know it's going to be over a month before I can get it fixed. I don't have any savings, and I can't draw unemployment because I'm self-employed. Looks like I've got some real problems.

So here I am unemployed, with a wife and four kids to feed, and a couple of broken ribs. The truck is only a year and a half old and about half paid for. I don't want the bank to take it back, so I guess I'll call my dad and see if he wants to take over the payments.

Dad says he will take over the truck. It's a pretty good deal for him, but I'm just happy to be out of it. We've been living paycheck to paycheck, and I've got about four hundred dollars in my pockets after the bills are paid. Things are looking kind of bleak. In case you have never been unemployed in Montana, let me tell you, there's not an abundance of jobs here.

I decide to go to Helena while I'm unemployed to see if there are any Federal jobs available. The man at the desk says they are taking applications for Air Traffic Controller positions now and also the U.S. Border Patrol, but you have to be a commercial pilot for the Air Traffic Controller position. I tell him, "I am a commercial pilot, and I would very much like to be an Air Traffic Controller."

He says, "Good, they'll be starting the exam in about an hour I'll sign you up for it." Then he says, "The Border Patrol exam will be given next week; are you interested in taking it also?"

I say, "What the hell is the Border Patrol?"

He hands me a brochure, and says, "You don't have anything to lose, might as well take it too."

I look at the brochure and say, "What do these people do anyway?"

"They patrol our borders," he says.

"Are they law enforcement officers?"

"Yes," he said.

"Wouldn't that be a kick in the ass if I was to become a federal officer after all these years of being an outlaw? Well, what the hell put me down to take the test next week? I guess I don't have anything to lose. Besides, there's an airplane on the front of the brochure, so it looks like the Border Patrol might have pilots. Maybe I'll be able to fly if I get in with the Border Patrol."

An hour later I go in and take the Air Traffic Controller test. The Air Traffic Control test is very straightforward, not easy, but simple to understand.

The next week I take the Border Patrol test. The Border Patrol test is also straightforward and easy to understand, except for the Mock Language portion. The Mock Language portion consists of questions and answers in a language invented solely for Border Patrol testing purposes. It has nouns, verbs, adjectives, adverbs, pronouns, etc., everything that other languages have, but I'm unable to pick out any of them, because they all look completely different. The language consists of its own alphabet, and the lettering is different. For someone that has a very good English background, or ability for foreign languages, it's probably quite simple to figure out. Unfortunately, that's not me; I can't even understand the directions. I'm the only applicant taking the test today; therefore, that guy at the front of the room giving the test and me are the only two people in the room. I guess I've got a strange look on my face, because the testing guy comes up to me and says, "Are you confused?"

"Confused hell, I don't have a clue as to what this part of the test is about."

He says, "Well, look here, for instance on question number one", and he reads the question and all the answers, and says; "Doesn't it look like answer B is the right answer?"

I look sideways at him and say, "Yes, it does, and what about question number two?" He reads question number two, and then he reads all the answers and says, "Now doesn't that look like it would be answer D?"

He goes through the entire Mock Language portion of the test with me. I'm glad he's here, because without him I know I couldn't pass this part of the test, giving me a much lower over-all score.

About two weeks go by and I am still unemployed. I'm down to my last dollars, but I finally find work with a logging outfit out of Idaho. I don't know anything about logging, but when they ask me I tell them, "Sure I do." I've run almost every kind of heavy equipment there is, so I think I can run a Skidder. (A Skidder is a 4-wheel drive tractor, or sometimes a crawler type tractor that is used to pull logs down off the mountain)

Well, it turns out that there are no Skidders at the job site yet, but I've told the bosses I can do anything, so they've asked me to fall timber instead. How can I refuse? I'm pretty sure I don't have them fooled, especially since I showed up out here wearing Hushpuppy shoes and no hard hat.

I don't know how I survive the first week, let alone an entire year, but I do. I sure get beat up by those trees. They almost kill me, but I manage to become a pretty good Timber Faller.

The results come back on those tests about a month after I took them. I wind up with a ninety one percent on the Air Traffic Control test and a ninety two percent on the United States Border Patrol test; with the additional five veteran's preference points, the scores are ninety six and ninety seven percent respectively.

Those are pretty good scores. It's been about a year now and I haven't heard a thing yet. I'd have thought I would have heard something by now. Guess I'll give them a call. You'd think they'd be real excited about hiring me with scores like that wouldn't you? I've been calling, and calling, and calling. I haven't been able to get in touch with anyone from the ATC sector, which is where I really want to go to work.

I do get in touch with the Border Patrol without too much of a problem. I ask the man that answers the phone why I haven't heard anything from them. I say, "It's been over a year since I took the test?"

He says, "Well, if you didn't get a hundred percent without veteran's preference, you might as well forget it. There are five thousand applicants for every job available, so even when we're hiring, the chances of getting on are very slim, and right now there is a hiring freeze."

Well, that does it - I'm going back to work in the woods. Life goes on for another two years.

My wife Jackie and I have just returned from Canada. We've been up there checking out the logging opportunities that I've been hearing about. Looks pretty good - I think I'll try to emigrate to Canada. I cut timber for a couple of days up there, and I'm very impressed with the amount of money I should be able to make. The logging contractors up there are very impressed with me. They tell me they will do everything they can to help me immigrate to Canada. I'm ready to go.

When we arrive at our home back in Montana we find a large stack of mail awaiting us. In that stack of mail is a letter from the Border Patrol. Well, look at this! It's the torn off corner of a piece of legal paper, and it says: “Are you still interested in the Border Patrol? If so, call this number."

It's the number of the Spokane Border Patrol Sector Headquarters. I look at it and laugh. I show it to Jackie, and we both laugh. I say, "What is this, some kind of joke".

"I don't think so", Jackie says.

"Well, if they can't afford a whole sheet of paper to notify me, to hell with them", I say, and I wad up the paper and throw it in the garbage.

For about a ten minute period, neither one of us say anything. I'm making pretty good wages in the woods, but I don't have any benefits. I don't have any health insurance. I can't get life insurance because Timber Falling is considered the number one most dangerous job in the United States. We can't afford to go on vacation because I don't get paid when I'm not working. Also, the jobs are becoming more scarce in the woods.

"I think I better reconsider," I soon decide, "Give me that paper back, and I'll make that call in the morning."

I am scheduled for an oral interview in two weeks. I'm pretty anxious, and the time seems to be dragging by. Finally the day arrives.

There are supposed to be four people at the interview, but only two of us show up. The Chief Patrol Agent from the Spokane Sector is the one giving the interview. He makes it perfectly clear that I have very little hope of becoming a Border Patrol Agent. He is very careful not to offer any encouragement. He repeats what the guy at the Federal Employment Office told me: there are five thousand applicants for every job available, so I shouldn't get my hopes up.

"Well, that was a waste of time." I say, after getting out of the interview.

"I guess I might as well go back to the woods and forget about the Border Patrol."

In March of 1974, I receive a letter instructing me to go to the Helena VA Hospital for a physical exam. I wasn't worried about passing a physical: my blood pressure was perfect, my eyesight was excellent, and everything was perfect except my hearing. I had been running heavy equipment all my life, and at twenty three years of age, my hearing was so bad that I was completely baffled when I passed the hearing test to get into the Army. I always figured that I had done so badly on the test that the people grading the test thought I was faking and passed me anyway. In fact, I still don't see how it could have been any other way because they told me how to take the test after they closed the doors on the booth and I never heard a thing the entire time I was in that booth. Every once in a while I would push one of the buttons I had in each hand. I really didn't care one way or the other that time, but this time I do care and I'm worried.

The actual physical exam is really thorough, and that makes me very uncomfortable because I can just imagine what the hearing test is going to be like. If they give me a test like the one I had in Butte for my induction into the army, I will never pass it.

Most of the exam is given to me by a lady doctor, and she is good. Then a male doctor comes and takes me to a different exam room. He goes through most of the standard procedure all over again, checking my pulse, looking into my eyes with one of those instruments, and looking into my ears with a different instrument. Then he walks out of the room, just around the corner of the door, and he says in a low whisper, "Can you hear this?"

I say, "yes, I can."

He comes back into the room and tells me I passed the hearing test. You see, hearing low pitched sounds was never my problem; it is the high pitched sounds that I can't hear.

I luck out once again.

Two weeks later I receive notification from the Border Patrol that I have passed the physical exam, and that I am to report to El Paso, Texas on June 17, 1974.

CHAPTER 2

Into the Border Patrol

It's very early in the morning Sunday, June 16, 1974. Jackie, the kids, and I all take off for the airport in Missoula. It's a sad day because we all know I will not be seeing them again for about 5 months, if I'm lucky. It is also very scary for Jackie because we don't have any extra money, and she will have to get by on what I make at the Academy. We know that will be much less than what I have been making in the woods.

After all the hugs and kisses, and the teary good-byes, I get on the airplane, destination El Paso, finally arriving about 10:00 P.M. It's been a long day.

I am able to find a motel near the airport, and after taking my suitcases to my room, I get the motel shuttle bus driver, to take me to find something to eat. He takes me to Sambo's; by now I'm starving. While I'm eating, a bunch of uniformed officers come in the door. They're so disheveled I can't help staring at them. They've got mud all over their shoes and dirt covering their uniforms. Their uniforms are pretty old, not torn, but well worn. Some are wearing baseball caps, and some are wearing straw hats. Generally speaking, they're a pretty raggedy looking group.

As they walk by, I can clearly see United States Border Patrol printed on their badges and shoulder patches. My God, what am I getting myself into, I think. I used to dress better than that when I was working in the woods.

Their appearance is really upsetting to me. All this time I have been picturing Border Patrol Agents just as they appeared on the brochure. What I'm looking at is definitely not that picture.

On the brochure agents were shown in their dress uniforms, including Smokey Bear hats. I can't believe that these guys are Federal Agents, but they are. I think about going back home. Then I think about all the money I have already spent to get here, and I decide that maybe I'd better stay a while.

On Monday at 8:00A.M., I report in at Sector Headquarters. Sure enough, I see a large gathering of those guys. They look a little better in the light of day. Maybe it's because they are going to work, instead of getting off. In fact, some of them are even in their dress uniforms. I guess the guys I had seen the night before had probably been working the Freight Yards, a fact that I came to find out later, and it's impossible to stay clean working around those trains.

The entire week I spend signing in, filling out paper work, doing orientation, being measured for uniforms, leather goods, etc. It requires more paper work to get into the Border Patrol than it does to get into the Army. It also costs a lot more money for uniforms.

During the orientation I find out a lot more about my future home, El Paso, Texas. Living here is really going to be a culture shock for my family and me, going from the green, lush mountains of Montana to the barren desert of West Texas.

El Paso is also a very big city, compared to what we're used to. There are almost as many people living in the city of El Paso as there are in the entire state of Montana. I wonder and worry about how my family will react when they arrive. It really is hot, and this isn't even the hottest part of the year yet.

CHAPTER 3

The Academy

Those of us that are going to fly have been issued airplane tickets to Harlingen, Texas, which is the closest airport to Port Isabel, Texas, where the Border Patrol Academy is located.

Port Isabel is located almost as far south and almost as far east as you can go in Texas. It isn't the end of the world, but you can see it from here. It is just as hot here as it was in El Paso, but it is also humid, very humid.

Being a Montana boy, I'm just not used to this kind of heat. I'm about to find out that there are a lot of things I'm not used to here: the bugs, the heat, reading, writing, and speaking Spanish-I'm not used to any of that. I guess if I'm going to last very long here, I'd better get used to it.

The academy issues our law books Sunday night and tells us to have them put together by Monday morning. There are three law books, and one Border Patrol Handbook. The books are loose-leaf binders with a large box of inserts that has to be gone through, put in order, and then put in the binders. The Handbook is probably about five hundred to a thousand pages long. The law books are about fifteen hundred to two thousand pages each. It's a big job.

One of the trainees from El Paso, who used to be a Chief of Police somewhere in Oklahoma, took one look at all those inserts and went back to Oklahoma. I don't feel as if I have the luxury of that option, so Monday morning my books and I will be ready to go.

My first week at the Academy is going pretty well. I'm getting really good grades in everything. I'm thinking, "Man, this is really great." I'm even getting high grades in Spanish, in spite of the fact that the guy had to do the Mock Language part of the entry exam for me.

It's the end of the second week now and I'm not doing quite as well in Spanish, but I'm thinking I'm still doing OK.

However, by the end of the fourth week my grades just keep getting worse and worse.

I start out studying Law and Spanish equally, about two hours each, every night, after a full eight hours of classroom work. By the end of the third week I am studying Spanish four hours and Law two hours. At the end of the fourth week I decide to devote a full eight hours to Spanish and nothing to Law. Fortunately, I'm not having a problem with Law.

The instructors are telling me they give a mid-term exam half way through the Academy, at the end of about seven weeks, in all subjects. These subjects include Law, Spanish, Physical Training, and Firearms Training.

These Mid-term Exams carry a lot of weight. If you are failing a subject, and you pass the exam, the Academy will probably keep you. At least they will keep you until they can determine whether you are going to continue to improve, if not you will be sent home. If you're failing a subject and you fail the exam, they will almost surely let you go.

That's where I am. I'm failing Spanish miserably. My grade average has dropped from about a ninety percent at the end of the second week to about sixty five percent now. There isn't any doubt in my mind that if I don't pass the Mid-term, I'm out of here. I have to come up with a different method of studying.

I'm nearly thirty six years old, and I've been out of school for about sixteen years, so I have completely forgotten how to study. I've been trying to learn everything there is to know about the Spanish language.

I'm going to try something different. I'm going to memorize all the questions and answers on all of my previous tests. I'm surprised it doesn't take nearly as much time or effort as I thought it would. In fact, it doesn't take as much time as studying all that material I was studying.

This new method of studying seems to pay off because I pass the Mid-term, not by much, but I pass. My score is seventy six. My grades after that just keep getting better and better.

Another thing I'm having a lot of problems with is that I'm so muscle bound from working in the woods all that time that I have a hard time moving fast. My legs are like steel. Every time I have to do wind sprints, my muscles just tear apart. We do wind sprints every day, so my muscles never get a chance to rebuild.

Going up and down stairs is a challenge. It's very painful, but my biggest problem is my hands. They are so stiff; they're almost arthritic from holding a chain saw all those years. Writing fast is impossible. I don't say anything to anyone, because it wouldn't do any good anyway, but not being able to write fast gives me a huge handicap on tests. No matter how fast the answers come to me, it seems to take forever to get them down on paper.

The last couple of weeks of training involves some field training. The first time out I go to work in the grapefruit and orange groves around McAllen. I'm very happy to be leaving the classroom and going to do some real Border Patrol work. We travel by van from the Academy to Brownsville, then on to Harlingen, and finally on to McAllen.

We make a stop at the Gateway Bridge in Brownsville to drop off some trainees. After we stop, I notice a lot of people leaning over the bridge railing, yelling, whistling, and pointing at the river. We all get out of the van and go to see what's happening. When we get close enough to the river, we can see several people out in the water. As soon as they reach our side of the river and start coming up out of the water, we can see that some of them have taken off some of their clothes to keep from getting them wet. There is one really fine looking Mexican lady who has taken off all of her very nice clothes. Needless to say, they can't get us back into the van till she puts them ALL back on.

We all agree that this is going to be a fantastic job, and we're all volunteering to work the Gateway Bridge. Our assignments have already been given however, so it is on to McAllen for me.

When we reach the McAllen Sector Headquarters, we go to roll call. We're assigned partners for the evening and given our assignments, and then we go to coffee.

At coffee we get to know each other a little bit and find out more about what is expected of us. The journeymen tell us to stick close to them because most of us can't speak Spanish very well. (But they also say that whenever we see someone run, we should catch him.)

When we get to the groves, it's pretty much see somebody run, catch him-see somebody run, catch him. By the end of the night, we have several vanloads of aliens, but we are told it is nothing unusual.

The next time out, I go to Harlingen. It's on a Monday. There aren't enough journeymen to go around, so I have to share one with Pete Vinton. Vinton is also going to be stationed in El Paso. Vinton is hung over from a weekend of drinking; actually he is still drunk. I don't know the journeyman's name, but he and Vinton share the same belt size.

We've been patrolling out in the country for about 30 minutes when Pete says, "I'm getting sick", and promptly vomits in the back seat. I think I'm going to be sick myself. The journeyman is madder than hell and now I'm riding with a drunk, and a pissed off journeyman. This field training seems to be getting off on the wrong foot. We're traveling down the levee, pretty slowly, when all of a sudden the journeyman slams on the brakes, slides to a stop, jumps out of the car, draws his pistol, and fires across the top of the car.

Pete vomits out the other side of the car. The journeyman says, "God damn it, I missed", and he fires again.

I'm looking out the right window in the direction he has been shooting. I see two tractors working a field, with a hawk circling over-head. I think, my God, I don't believe what I'm seeing here-a federal officer shooting at a hawk, with two tractors working right below it.

Fortunately the tractors keep going straight down the furrow, and they still seem to be under control. Pete is still hanging halfway out the door, vomiting. I'm making deals with God to get me through this night without being fired.

The prayers seem to work because I do make it through the night and I don't get fired.

In addition to the Academy, the McAllen Sector Detention Center is also located at the Bayview Facility. We're allowed an interview with some of the illegal aliens that are housed there during the last two weeks of training. We go over to the Detention Center, pick out the aliens we want to talk to, sit across the table from them, and interview them.

Yeah, right! They're speaking Spanish very well; we're speaking English very well. We're also learning to use sign language pretty well. You see, even though we can read and write Spanish pretty well we haven't really learned to speak Spanish yet.

I don't think the Border Patrol really expects us to interview the aliens. I think they just want us to know what we we're in for when we get back to our duty stations. Do these instructors really think we need something more to worry about?

Eighteen and a half weeks is a long time to be away from my wife and family. Jackie is struggling to keep things together back in Montana. She's selling things to keep food on the table, like the freezer, furniture that we can get by without, chain saws, etc.. I don't know whether there will be anything left to take to El Paso by the time I get back home.

Finally, it's graduation time. I make it. There are about twenty guys out of about a hundred and fifteen that don't make it. The rest of us are ready to get the ceremony out of the way and head for home; or at least I am.

Two of the trainees that are stationed at El Paso have been going out with a couple of young women that work at the Hanger Club in Harlingen. The guys are both married, but they probably haven't thought to mention that part to the girls. After all, the wives are so far away, and they're going to El Paso and will never see these girls again anyway. So what difference does it make, right?

They invite the girls to graduation, and sure enough here they are, sitting right in the front row. We're all getting our group pictures taken and getting ready to start the ceremony, when lo and behold the wives of these two agents walk in and sit down in the front row, right next to the girlfriends.

I guess they're here to surprise their husbands, and they sure have. They wave at their husbands, and the husbands hesitantly wave back. The girlfriends look at the wives, and I hear a little buzz of conversation begin among the trainees.

I'm almost sorry that I'm leaving immediately after the ceremony, but I have to, in order to make my flight. Things are going to get interesting.

I'm really eager to get home, so, of course, the airplane breaks down in Dallas. That makes me late for my flight out of Denver. The next flight isn't till the following morning, so the airline puts me up over night. I call home, but Jackie has already left for the airport in Missoula, and there isn't any way to get in touch with her. I leave a message for her if she calls home. Then I call the airport in Missoula and leave a message for her there. It's all I can do.

It's a long night in Denver, and I'm really getting anxious now. Finally, I arrive in Missoula. There she is standing at the gate. My God, she's beautiful. She has reserved a motel room for us. We're not going home tonight. Wow! What a beautiful woman. We spend the rest of the day, and night at the motel before going home. I'm in heaven.

I've got twelve days to get from the Academy, back to Montana, and then down to El Paso. When I get home, I have ten days left. I'll have to make arrangements to sell my mobile home, rent a U-Haul truck, pack everything we own, drive the sixteen hundred and ten miles from Deer Lodge, Montana to El Paso, Texas, find a place to live in El Paso, unload the U-Haul, and return it. A piece of cake.

Lucky for me, my brother Gary isn't doing anything else right now, and he volunteers to help us move. We'll make it, even though it doesn't seem like it right now.

When we arrive in El Paso, we have to stay in a motel for about a week while we look for a house. Can you imagine what it's like in a motel with four kids, a dog, a cat, and three adults? We find a house in three days. We are almost moved in by the time I start work.

CHAPTER 4

On The Job

I start work as a trainee in El Paso today, November 4, 1974. Actually my first day was yesterday, Sunday, November 3, but this is my first day on duty. I'm working the day shift with a guy named Lester Franks. We're covering the Ascarate Park area, and so far we've caught a few Mexicans trying to enter the United States illegally. They all just give up and get in the vehicle. We're on our way to the Paso Del Norte (PDN) Bridge, where the Border Patrol maintains a holding cell and a write-up area.

We arrive at the bridge, and Lester grabs several Standard Form I-213's. Information on the form includes name, date of birth, place of birth, height, weight, hair color, where and how they crossed the river into the U.S., mother and father's names, etc.. This speaking and understanding Spanish is the hard part. I stutter, stammer, and wrack my brain for the correct words to ask these questions.

It seems like its taking hours for me to write up my share of the aliens. We caught six, so my share is three. Lester finishes his easily, and now he's just sitting there watching me. Whenever I get really stuck, he helps me, but I have to ask for it, and even then he only gives me hints.

I've been thinking for a while now that I'm going to have to sleep here. The situation I'm in here seems to be fun for everyone but me. For instance, when I ask the first one his name, (In Spanish, "Como se llama" means, "What is your name?" or literally, "How are you called?"), I make the mistake of asking, "Como me llamo?" which means, "What's my name?" Everybody's laughing, which makes me even more self-conscious. Even the aliens are laughing. It's a good thing that these are just simple Entry Without Inspection's (EWI's), and not smuggling cases, or I might be here for my entire career with these three aliens.

Tuesday is a post academy training day. Every Tuesday and Friday, from this day on, until the five and a half month exams are given, will be devoted to training, Spanish and law, after that it will be every Thursday until the ten month exams.

Up until now we've had minimal training as far as speaking Spanish is concerned. The Post Academy Training is devoted almost entirely to speaking Spanish; of course, there are the law courses as well. We will have exactly one month to get prepared for the five and a half month exams. I spend most of that time processing illegal aliens at the PDN Bridge.

I don't feel as if I'm getting much better at it, but I keep trying. I'm still having a lot of trouble with my hands; they're just too stiff to write fast enough, and I know there isn't anyone who would buy that excuse, so I just keep plugging away.

Where has all the time gone? Here it is December 3, the day we all take the Law Exam. I'm not worried about law; I'll pass that with flying colors. A few of the guys have pretty low grades, but they will probably pass. I think there's only one guy that might fail the Law Test.

Sure enough we all pass except for one, and nobody expected him to pass.

December 5, is Spanish Exam day. The manner in which agents are tested goes like this: You have a couple of Chief Patrol Agents or at least one Chief Patrol Agent, and one Assistant Chief Patrol Agent that do the testing. One of the two plays the part of the illegal alien, and the other one monitors the testing and reviews the evaluations done by the journeymen agents on the trainee. The one that plays the illegal alien does not speak anything but Spanish after the testing has begun, and the other one does not speak at all. If you have any questions concerning the test, they have to be asked in Spanish and answered in Spanish.

The test itself contains forty questions, plus the jurat (an affidavit, by the officer, showing by whom, when, and before whom it was sworn to). The jurat should take about three to four minutes to read, if there are no mistakes. If there are mistakes, you have to go back and correct them, and that takes precious time.

The first twenty questions are the questions from the Form I-213, which I've explained above. These questions are pretty familiar to me by this time and not nearly as difficult as the second set of twenty questions that come after the jurat is read. These questions pertain to a smuggling case, and almost anything can be expected to appear in these questions.

The questions themselves are written in English and are to be translated into Spanish. The answers are given in Spanish and are to be recorded in English below the questions.

The jurat is written in English and is to be translated into Spanish. The exam must be completed in one hour. If there is one word in the question that I do not know, I will not be able to ask the question. If I'm unable to ask the question, I will not get an answer. So if that should happen I will lose both the question and the answer.

I don't suppose it's possible, but the testing seems like both the longest and the shortest hour I have ever spent in my life.

When the hour is up, I go out in the hall and wait for the testing officers to grade the test. Thirty minutes later they called me back in, have me sit down, and tell me I have failed the test.

That's right; I got a sixty eight. They tell me it will be up to the Chief Patrol Agent to decide whether I stay or go. They tell me he will probably take into consideration the grade on my Law Exam, the evaluations made by the journeymen agents that I have worked with, and the report given to him by the post academy training officers.

There are about five of us that did not pass the test. Most of us are in about the same boat, except for Trainee Binder; he failed both tests. The officers terminate him on the spot. Binder has been a member of the United States Capitol Police Corp, and he's made the statement many times that they cannot fire him because he has already obtained journeyman status.

He's been given two weeks notice and a recommendation to the U.S. Customs Service. They tell me he will be hired right away, that it happens routinely. When the Border Patrol terminates a trainee for failure to pass the exams, the trainee is almost always picked up by U.S. Customs or by the U.S. Immigration Service.

Many people believe the U.S. Border Patrol and the U.S. Immigration Service is one and the same. They are not. They are, along with DEA and the FBI, individual agencies under the Department Of Justice.

The Immigration Service operates the U.S. Ports Of Entry. The U.S. Border Patrol covers all of the areas between the Ports Of Entry.

In other words, if you come into the U.S. legally or illegally through one of the Ports Of Entry, or if you apply for citizenship or resident alien status, you will talk to an Immigration Inspector. If you attempt to come in illegally, without going through a Port Of Entry, a Border Patrol Officer will arrest you (This is how it was in 1974, today they are all under the Homeland Security).

It's been a week now since the test, and I'm being called into Chief Nelson's Office. I'm in uniform, with my nametag in full view.

He asks me, "What is your name?"

I look down at my name-tag to make sure it's still there, and I say "Darryl Rambo."

"Are you married," he says.

I look down again to see if I have lost my wedding ring, nope it's still there.
"
Yes sir, I'm married."

"Do you have any children?"

"Yes, sir, I have four children."
"Well, Mr. Rambo, it doesn't look to me as though you're trying very hard."

I stand ramrod straight, look him square in the eye, and say nothing, but I'm thinking, You stupid son-of-a-bitch, I've dragged my family 1600 miles, put everything I have on the line, spent 5 months at the academy without seeing my family, and you say I'm not trying. You have all my paper work in front of you, but you obviously haven't looked at it, or you would know my name and know that I am married and have four children.

He went on, "I'd think a man with a wife and family would put out a little effort to try to keep this job, or maybe you don't care if you keep this job. Is that it, Mr. Rambo?"

"No, Sir, I want very much to keep this job."

"Well, Mr. Rambo, if you expect to keep this job, you're going to have to put out a lot more effort than you have been doing."

"Yes, Sir, I've already hired a tutor to help me with my Spanish."

"If you don't show a lot of improvement within a very short time, Mr. Rambo, we're going to have to let you go. Your post academy instructor, Mr. Simons will keep me posted. Good day, Mr. Rambo."

"Good day, Sir."

OK! I'm not terminated, so it's back to work I go. My tutor's name is Mrs. Esperanza, and she was a Spanish Instructor at the U.S.B.P. Academy when it was located in El Paso many years ago. She's very good and gives me a lot more personal attention than I'm getting from the post academy training course.

I'm going to see Mrs. Esperanza twice a week now for two hours, and the post academy is still twice a week. It's getting to be a pretty busy schedule.

The job is becoming more interesting though, as I progress. The more I'm able to speak to the people, the easier and the more interesting the work becomes. I'm finding that almost everyone has a sad story and a very good reason for coming into the United States.

Of course, it doesn't make any difference; I still have to put illegal aliens back across the border because they don't have the proper paper work. Stepping on peoples dreams like this is very difficult for me, even though what they are doing is illegal.

When I first entered the Border Patrol, I did not believe in borders. I only took the job because it offered a lot more security than I had in the woods. I used to feel that people should be able to go wherever they want to go and not have to worry about imaginary lines in the sand. I've been having a real struggle with my integrity.

I've given it a great deal of thought lately, and I'm changing my mind. If we lived in an ideal world, there would be no need for borders, but we do not. We have all different kinds of governments throughout the world. Some governments are very oppressive; some are very liberal, etc.. If the people in these other countries want the kind of life we have in the USA, they will have to fight for it, just as our ancestors fought for ours, and we have fought to preserve it. If that means revolution in their countries, so be it; it's what had to happen here. Whatever happens, the change has to take place in their country, or nothing will ever change. We cannot continue to take these people in forever; even our country is not big enough for that.

Another thing that should be considered is we have a very liberal immigration quota. If we allow people to come in illegally it is not fair to those who apply to immigrate legally. It takes several years, in some cases, for those who apply legally to ever get into the U.S., to even start their residency requirements. If we allow those who come in illegally to just remain here and eventually become citizens without due process, where is the justice in that?

The job is becoming a lot clearer, since I've worked those little details out. Even though it is clear, it still is not easy, and I know that if I were south of that border, I would be doing the very same thing they are doing. I also know though, that if the situation were reversed, they would be doing the same thing I am.

This whole people hunting experience is becoming a game for me, and although it is a life struggle for them, they also consider it a game. Most of them know that if they want into the U.S. bad enough, and if they will just keep trying, eventually they will make it. Whenever they are caught, many of them say, "Pues, mala suerte," which means, "Well, bad luck," and they will try again tomorrow. So let the games begin.

CHAPTER 5

First Court Case

Nothing exciting has happened since the exams. It's about four days before Christmas, and my partner John Mohler and I are ready to go home. We are at the PDN write-up room when we get a call informing us that there is a car parked on the bank of the river just west of the head-gates area. This is our assigned area, and no other agents have relieved us yet, so we respond immediately.

We have a night vision scope with us, so we head for the University of Texas at El Paso (UTEP) parking lot, where we will be able to observe the area where the car is parked without being detected. We set up in the parking lot, and we can see the vehicle and the people very clearly. There are four of them, all males, and they are just milling around the car. They all seem to be drinking something. They have another larger bottle that they're passing around. We are assuming they are drinking beer and passing around a bottle of whisky or tequila.

The car is an older model Chevy, maybe a 68 or 69 model, and the door on the luggage compartment is wide open. We watch for about ten or fifteen minutes, and then we notice a couple of guys wading across the river. The river is only about three feet deep, so it isn't hard for them to do. They come up to the people with the car and seem to be talking with them and having a couple of drinks. We can't tell whether they've brought anything across with them, but they all keep hanging around the open luggage compartment.

After about twenty minutes the two guys wade back across the river and disappear. The guys at the car close the luggage compartment, get in the car, and take off to the east. We shut down the night scope, jump in our car, and race to intercept them. When we're almost to the bottom of the Yandell Street. overpass, we spot the car we've been watching. It turns onto the Yandell overpass going the opposite direction, so we have to continue to the bottom of the overpass, turn around, and catch it. The guys aren't driving real fast, so we catch them right away.

We have them pull off to the side of the street and stop. Once they are stopped, we pull in behind them and get out of our car. My partner approaches the driver's side of their car, and I stand at the right rear fender where I have a clear view of the inside of the vehicle. I've drawn my revolver, and I'm holding it at my side just in case they're armed.

John asks them where they're from, and they all answer, "El Paso".

"Where were you born", John asks?

"El Paso", they all say. They're all United States citizens, and they are all very drunk. John asks the driver to open the trunk.

"I can't open the trunk", he says.

“You can open the trunk, and you will open the trunk," John says.

“No sir, I'm serious, I cannot open the trunk," he says. "I do not have a key."

"Where is the key?"

"I was at a party a couple of days ago, and I lost the key".

"Well, I don't care how you open it. Just open it. Or maybe you would rather we open it. We have a tire wrench in the car that I'm sure will open it", says John.

"No, I can take out the back seat, and get in that way".

We know he can open it because it was open down by the river. We figure if he wants to make a game out of it, we'll let him.

Meanwhile one of the guys in the back seat is making quite a scene. He's a big, blond haired, blue-eyed Hispanic and very boisterous. He does not like gringos, he does not like border patrolmen, and he especially does not like gringo border patrolmen.

He comes stumbling out of the back seat of the car screaming, "I have my rights man. You are violating my rights man. I will have your jobs man".

He comes right at me, and he is bigger than I thought. He's about six foot five inches tall, and weighs about two hundred and twenty five pounds. When he comes at me, I raise my gun up because it's the only thing I have to hit him with, and he's too big for me to wrestle with.

My partner sees what I'm doing and yells, "Don't shoot; don't shoot." Of course, I have no intentions of shooting him, but John doesn't know that. Melendez, the big blond Hispanic, doesn't know that either, so he makes a right turn and heads for John. That's a mistake because John is just as big as Melendez, and John hasn't been drinking. John stretches him out over the trunk lid and holds him there until he shuts up.

I have the other three sit on the sidewalk, so I can handle them. John tells Melendez to sit down with his friends, and he turns to go to the car to call the city police. When John turns his back, Melendez tries to attack him again, but his three friends hold him back. When John gets on the radio, Melendez breaks away from his friends and takes off running down the street. I can't chase him because I have the other three to watch, so John takes off in the car to chase him. They come back a few minutes later with Melendez leaking a little bit of blood from a small cut on his head where he hit the sidewalk when John tackled him. He isn't any quieter, but at least he's handcuffed and in the back seat of the patrol car.

We get the other three up and tell them to start taking the rear seat out of the car. It takes about fifteen minutes. The driver is able to open the trunk from the inside; I don't know how he does it. I guess there's an inside latch on this model car. When he gets it open, there isn't anything in it, not even a spare tire. So we tell the three guys who haven't given us any trouble to put it back together and be on their way. We tell them we're going to keep their friend, and we were going to charge him with disorderly conduct when the police arrive. They close the trunk, put the seat back in, and leave.

We wait for nearly a half hour, but the police never do arrive, so we take Melendez over to the jail ourselves. All the way up the stairs, and into the booking room, he's yelling about his rights and how we're picking on him and how he's going to sue us. When we finally get him booked, and put him in the cell, a transformation like I've never seen before takes place. When that cell door goes CLANGGGGG, he actually falls to his knees, and starts crying. I mean great big sobs. He says, "I'm sorry, mister. I'll never do that again. Please, mister, don't lock me up in here." We can still hear him crying as we descend the stairs leaving the building.

The next day we appear in court at 8:00 P.M. The judge asks us what has taken place, and Mohler, being the senior officer, tells him what happened, just as it's written above. Then he asks me if that's the way I saw it, and I say, "Yes, Sir."

He turns to Melendez and says, "What do you have to say for yourself Mr. Melendez?"

Mr. Melendez looks at the judge, who happens to be Hispanic, probably thinking he will be more sympathetic toward him, and says, "I didn't do any of those things they say I did. They're just picking on me because I am a Mexican. They say I was drunk, but I only had about two beers."

The judge asks, "Were you born in Mexico, Mr. Melendez?"

"No."

"Were you born in the United States, Mr. Melendez?"

"Yes."

"Then you are an American, Mr. Melendez. Were you alone in the car Mr. Melendez?"

"No, there were three other guys with me."

"Where are they Mr. Melendez?"

"I don't know, Judge; I guess they're at home."

"Were the other three guys Anglos, Mr. Melendez?"

"No, they were Mexi, I mean, Americans just like me."

"Well, Mr. Melendez, it seems strange to me that there were four Hispanic males in the car, but you are the only one picked on for being Hispanic. I find you guilty of disorderly conduct, and I'm going to fine you fifty dollars, or give you five days in jail. Do you have fifty dollars, Mr. Melendez?"

"No, but my girlfriend does, I think. Can I talk to her?"

"Is she in the courtroom?"

"Yes."

"Have her come forward, Mr. Melendez."

A young lady comes forward and the judge asks her, "Do you wish to pay this man's fine, young lady?"

"Yes, Your Honor." .

"Very well, case dismissed."

I guess it doesn't amount to much, but it's my first time being on the prosecution side, and I find it very interesting.

CHAPTER 6

Poetic Justice

Everywhere the flowers are blooming, trees are beginning to bud, and a new crop of grass is poking out of the ground. Little birds are hatching; baby rabbits and fawns are trying out their little legs. It's springtime across the land.

In El Paso, Texas, the wind is blowing about ninety miles per hour, and the back yards are filled with tumbleweeds that have blown in over the fence. It has been a long day, a very long day. Any day working with Agent Tough Boy Sanchez is a long day. He can get into more trouble by accident than most people can on purpose. We are tired, and our eyes are filled with sand. We decide that we are going to get off on time for a change, and we're headed for the station. We're working the 8:00 A.M. to 4:00 P.M. shift, and it's a quarter to four. The children are getting out of school.

We are traveling east on Alameda Street, and Tough Boy is driving. We stop for a red light at Second Street. I'm kind of scooched down in the passenger seat, blankly looking out the right side window toward the ground. I'm trying not to see anything because if I do see something, we'll never get off on time. A car pulls up in the right lane next to us. I'm really not paying any attention, but it's hard not to notice that beat-up right front fender and that right front tire that's as smooth as a baby's behind. I let my tired eyes wander back across the lines of that vintage model Chevy, still not paying much attention, but thinking it really is a mess. There are three guys in the car. As my eyes pass over the driver, I notice that he is Hispanic, hasn't shaved for about a week, has long black stringy hair that hasn't seen a comb since the day that car was new, and he is ugly. I mean BUTT ugly. He has a mean, surly look on his face, and the middle finger of his left hand is extended toward me in that time-honored salute. He punches it; with tires smoking he goes right through that red light.

I say, "Awww, Shiiiit."

Tough Boy says, "God Dammit, I really wanted to get off on time".

We turn on the overheads, and the chase is on.

Tough Boy looks both ways and runs that red light right behind him. We're going about seventy miles per hour down Alameda Street, and he's pulling away from us. We don't want to go any faster because even though Alameda is a wide, five-lane street, there are children going home from school, and it's just too dangerous. I call the El Paso PD, inform them of the situation, give them our location, and ask for their assistance. About that time "Ole Ugly" makes a hard right turn onto a side street. For a minute it looks like he is going turn the car over but then it settles back down on all four wheels again. He only goes about a half a block before he makes a hard left turn into a vacant lot, still going very fast. The vacant lot is unpaved dirt with tumbleweeds and right next to a school.

There is a high chain link fence between the vacant lot and the school.

We're becoming increasingly nervous, and “Ole Ugly” is becoming increasingly reckless. Tumble weeds and sand are flying thirty feet in the air, as Ugly makes a couple of loops around the vacant lot. We're still right behind him. He exits the lot and heads south on the side street. After about three blocks, he makes another right turn onto a very narrow street. There are cars parked all along this street, and it is impossible to tell if there's anyone between them. If someone steps out from between those cars he or she will be killed for sure. Ugly is going about fifty miles per hour and still accelerating.

Tough Boy says, "That’s it. I guess he's going to get away, but I'm not going to chase him any further. If we keep after him, he's going to kill somebody."

We continue on down the street, but at a much slower pace. We see the car make another high speed right turn about three or four blocks ahead of us, and we can see the dust flying as it did at the vacant lot. When we get to the corner, we find the car upside down, smashed against a rock wall, wheels still spinning and dust just starting to settle. Tough Boy and I look at each other and shrug our shoulders, and both of us say at the same time, "Well, we got him stopped." We get out to see how bad it is.

It's hard to tell at first what the situation really is. Things are pretty well scrambled inside that car. Both of the passengers seem to be OK, but we can't tell about the driver. The rear seat passenger is a young man about sixteen years old, and he says he's all right.

Tough Boy asks him where he was born. This is the first question any Border Patrol Officer should ask in a situation like this, because if we are not concerned about their citizenship, then we have no reason to be chasing them.

He says, "El Paso."

"Where do you live?"

"Right down the street about five blocks."

The front seat passenger is about twenty five years old, six foot one or two inches tall, weighs about two hundred pounds, and is crying his eyes out.

He says, "I try to make heem slow down, man. I toll heem he wuss gone to keel sumbudy, man. I toll heem he wuss gone to keel us, man. He woodn't leesten, man. I theenk he's crazy. Jew know what I mean"?

I go around to the driver's side.

Now this is something I didn't expect. What a surprise. The driver is just a little shrimp. I mean I don't think he's over four foot ten inches tall, and I'll bet he doesn't weigh ninety pounds. He's probably about twenty eight or twenty nine years old. He has broad shoulders, and he must have been sitting on a box or something when he was driving because he appeared to be a fairly large guy when he was sitting behind the wheel. Of course, he's still ugly, but he sure doesn't look very mean anymore. Just like his front seat passenger, he's crying too.

"Pleese, man. I deedn't went to hurd enybody. I wuss juss foolin arown, man. I deedn't mean anything, man. I'm sorry I fleep jew off, man".

He has a small cut on his forehead, and he doesn't seem to be able to move his legs. He's dragging himself out of the car through the driver's window. I take hold of his shoulders and help him out of the car. When he's completely out, I can see that the lower half of his body is all shriveled up. He's completely paralyzed from the waist down.

There are several empty beer bottles in the car, and it smells like a brewery. He tells me the reason he lost control of the vehicle is that he missed the brake with the stick and hit the gas pedal instead.

I say, "What do you mean, you missed the brake with the stick; what stick are you talking about?"

He says, "Thees steek," and he reaches in the car and pulls out an ordinary one by two inch stick about three foot long. He says, "Me legs don work, man, so I yoos thees steek to poosh thee paydels".

Oh lordy, am I glad there weren't any children unfortunate enough to have stepped out in front of that vehicle. Can you picture it, a ninety pound invalid, drunk on his ass, sitting on a box, using a stick to operate the gas and brake pedals, driving seventy miles per hour, weaving in and out of traffic, running stop signs and red lights, and school children all over the streets.

The El Paso PD shows up at that time. The officers ask us what has taken place. We tell them. They ask us if we want these guys for anything, and we tell them no. Tough Boy says, "We just wanted to ask the young man in the back seat what his citizenship is. He told us he's a United States citizen. That's all we need."

We volunteer to give the young man a ride home if they don't need him for anything. They tell us to go ahead and give him a ride. On the way to his home we give him a little lecture on the kind of company he's keeping. When we get to his home, Tough Boy tells his parents what has happened, and we leave.

As we're pulling away, Tough Boy says, "Poetic Justice isn't it wonderful".

"Yep, my granddad always said, ‘Never judge a book by its cover;’ now I know what he meant."

CHAPTER 7

Crazy Mary

It's the second week of April the wind has let up, and it's just a nice, balmy spring day. I'm working the East Railroad Bridge area with my journeyman partner, Frank Westly. There's another agent working the West Railroad Bridge, Don Hart. Now Frank is a real serious guy most of the time; in fact, there aren't very many people in the El Paso Sector that know Frank has a sense of humor.

First of all, let me tell you about the West Railroad Bridge. It is known throughout the Border Patrol and most of Mexico by its Mexican name, El Puente Negro, which means The Black Bridge. The reason for its being called The Black Bridge is that it's a bridge and it's black-nothing more. The West Railroad Bridge is owned by the Sante Fe Railroad and is used for access into Mexico. The same applies to El Puente Verde, The Green Bridge, owned by the Missouri Pacific Railroad that crosses the Rio Grande River about two blocks East of the Black Bridge. El Puente Verde does not share the notoriety of El Puente Negro. There are three reasons for this lack of notoriety location, location, and location. El Puente Negro crosses the river straight South of Chihuahua Street (pronounced Chee-wah-wah). The railroad tracks that cross the bridge run directly behind the Chihuahua Street apartments and straight into the Sante Fe Railroad Yards, located just slightly more than one block north of the bridge. Because of the way the freight yard is situated, it is very difficult to intercept anyone who is able to make it as far as the

Chihuahua Street Apartments, slightly over a half a block north of the bridge.

Most of the apartment residents are sympathetic to the illegal aliens, having been there themselves, and they are willing to hide the aliens from the Border Patrol. It's a strange love, hate, relationship they have with the Border Patrol. They hide the aliens, yet if they have any situations for which they should call the police or EMS, they don't; they call the Border Patrol.

Once the aliens have made it into the rail yards, they are able to hide themselves very well among the trains that are being put together. Switch engines are constantly taking a single box car or several box cars and moving them from one track to another. I think there are about sixteen sets of tracks in the Sante Fe Yards. Because of the constant activity in the yards and all of the railroad tracks that keep the BP agents from being able to drive through the yards, aliens think it's a very good place to cross into the U.S. The BP thinks it's a good idea to not let the aliens get as far as the apartments, so whoever is unfortunate enough to be assigned to the West Bridge generally stations him or herself between the bridge and the apartments and stays there for the entire shift.

For that reason, there are always anywhere from fifty to three hundred and fifty people on and around the bridge. They are continually attempting or feigning an attempt to get around the agent that is parked there. If the agent is foolish enough to give chase, he will leave a hole big enough for the entire three hundred and fifty people to enter.

It's a very frustrating job, and all of the agents hate drawing that assignment. Anyone assigned to work the East Bridge area is expected to help the agent at the West Bridge if he gets into trouble.

The East Bridge does not have much traffic at all, compared to the West Bridge. The reason for that is that the Missouri Pacific RR yard is located several blocks east of the bridge. Therefore, there are no more obstacles there to slow the BP agents down than there is anywhere else. Of course, directly across from the Missouri Pacific Yards is another story.

Between the two railroad bridges and well above them is the Paso Del Norte Bridge, a pedestrian and vehicular Port Of Entry into the U.S.A. Foot traffic going into Mexico has a very good view of the West Bridge, and foot traffic coming into the U.S. has a good view of the East Bridge.

On this particular day there are about three hundred and fifty people at the West Bridge. The bridge itself is completely covered with people. The banks of the river are concrete on both sides, and the concrete starts about a block west of the bridge and runs east all the way to Ysleta, about seven or eight miles. There are people down on the apron on both sides, sitting all along the rails at the top of the concrete banks on both sides, and all along the levee to the end of the concrete. Don Hart really has his hands full. Every once in a while someone will make it around him, and he'll call us to go catch him. Sometimes we catch him, sometimes we don't, but we try.

We've just finished doing the paperwork on a group of aliens, and we're leaving the PDN processing center when we hear a lot of cheering coming from the direction of the West Bridge. As soon as we're in the sedan, Frank calls Don and asks him what's going on.

He says, "You'll have to come see for yourself, I can't explain it over the air."

By the time we get there, it seems as if whatever was happening before is over. Frank notices a woman standing all by herself and points her out to me.

He says, "That's Mary I'll bet she's the one causing all the trouble."

That's all he says, no explanation, nothing. Well, she looks harmless enough to me. She's a petite, well-proportioned lady, wearing a loose fitting, knee length dress, and no shoes. She's probably forty, to forty five years old.

I say, "She doesn't look like a trouble maker to me. How much trouble can a little women like that cause?"

He says, "Just put her in the car, I'll tell you later."

"OK."

Frank stops the car about 20 feet away from Mary. I get out of the car and stroll over toward her. As I get close to her, I reach out with my left hand, and say, "Come on Mary, let's go." I've never seen anything like what happens next. One instant I'm looking at a woman standing in front of me fully clothed; the next instant I'm looking at a naked woman. It all happened so fast that I can't tell you how it happened. All I know is there she stands, naked as the day she was born, and her dress has become a belt. Somehow she has moved the top down and the bottom up and twisted it all into a belt that fit snuggly around her waist; she's also not wearing any under clothes. I turn beet red.

I look at Frank, and he's laughing his fool head off. The crowd is going wild. In addition to the three hundred and fifty aliens that are hanging around the West RR Bridge, there are about a hundred to a hundred and fifty citizens up above on the PDN Bridge. Everyone is roaring. I turn around, go back to the car, and sit down. I can see the handwriting on the wall, if I try to force her into the car things are just going to get worse.

From the car, I try to persuade her to come get in the car and go with us. I keep saying, "Vengase, Maria, y subase en el carro." ("Come Mary, and get in the car.") I keep asking her this over, and over. Once in a while I tell her, "Don't worry. We won't touch you; we just want some information, and we'll let you go back to Mexico."

All the while I'm pleading with her; she's walking east along the levee. All the while she's walking, the crowd is cheering. We pass under the PDN Bridge, and now we're about 100 yards east of the bridge. All at once Mary stops, puts her dress back in place, walks over to the car, opens the rear door on the passenger side, gets in, and sits down. She has decided the game is over.

Man, am I relieved. At last, the crowd is silent. I say, "Gracias, Maria."

"De nada," she replies.

When Mary walks through the door at the PDN, everybody cheers. They all know Maria. Now I know Maria.

There are many stories circulating about Maria. I don't know if any of them are true or not. One of the stories is that she became a U.S. citizen many years ago by marrying a Colonel in the U.S. Army. The Colonel was killed some time later, and she returned to Mexico. While she was in Mexico, she was gang raped by several Mexican soldiers; then later she was thrown in jail for prostitution. While in jail, she was raped by several of the guards. When the Mexicans finally let her out of jail, she had lost her mind. I know the last part is true, for she has definitely lost her mind. There isn't any way to know whether Maria is a citizen or not because she will never give her correct name, and like most illegal aliens, she never carries any identification. Maria is harmless though, and she never goes very far from the river. For that reason I vow that I will never arrest Maria again.

Since we're on the subject of Crazy Mary, let me jump ahead about a year and tell you about another story involving Mary.

I'm working the West Bridge again, and I've taken up a post at the end of Chihuahua Street. One of the new supervisors, George Figaroa, comes driving up alongside my vehicle. George was a journeyman when I first got to El Paso and was just promoted to supervisor about a month ago. We talk for a few minutes about how hot and how quiet it is. There doesn't seem to be much going on today, and I'm very thankful because that is very rare for the West Bridge. George drives away, and I go back to the book I'm reading. About five minutes later George calls me on the radio, "Hey, Rambo there is a woman at the base of the PDN Bridge. She looks like an illegal alien. Will you go pick her up?"

"Ten four, George, I'm on my way."

I drive over to the base of the bridge, and surprise, surprise-there stands Mary. I shake my finger at her and grin. She acts as if she's going to take her dress off and then shakes her finger at me and grins. I call George and tell him, "I don't see any illegal aliens here George."

He says, "She's there all right. She's standing right there on the west side of the street, and she's naked."

I could hear the frustration in his voice, but Maria has all her clothes on now, and I choose not to recognize her anyway, so I answer, "Sorry George, there aren't any naked women here." He says, "I know she's there, dammit; I just saw her."

"Sorry George, I can't find her. I'm going back to the bridge."

Now I know that George is calling from the PDN write-up room, and he has already told everyone in there that it’s Crazy Mary at the end of the bridge. So when I go in later to write up some aliens that I’ve caught, it’s no surprise to me when they tell me George had called from there, and he was so mad that he could hardly talk. They told me he stomped around in there for a half an hour, madder than a hornet.

I say, "Well, guys! If he saw her, he knew it was Crazy Mary, knew she was illegal, why didn't he pick her up himself? Instead, he drives right by her and calls me. Or do you suppose maybe he did try to pick her up, and that's when she got naked? At any rate, it's his problem, not mine."

Do you think maybe that's why some supervisors don't really care for me?

CHAPTER 8

Ten Months Exam

The time has finally arrived, ten months exam time. It's the time we have all been dreading, but at the same time we want to get it over with. We take the Law Exams first, just like last time.

It's Friday, April 18, 1975, and we're all seated and waiting for the test to begin. We're all tested at the same time. We're given explicit instructions on how to take the test and told to be sure to check our paperwork when we finish and make sure all of the questions are answered. When we are sure we have answered all the questions, we bring the test to the front of the room, deposit it on the desk, and leave the room quietly. We are told if we leave the room without answering all of the questions, we will not be allowed to re-enter and finish the test.

I am about a third of the way through the test when Weldon Hiatt takes his test to the front, deposits it on the desk, and leaves the room. I'm thinking, my God, that's impossible. How can he possibly finish the test so quickly? When I'm about two thirds of the way through, three other guys get up and leave. Just before I finish the test, Weldon comes back into the room and has a little discussion with the two post-academy instructors, Agents Jones and Simons. Then all of them have a little discussion with the Chief Patrol Agent that's conducting the test, Weldon soon sits down and finishes his test.

What has happened is that two of the pages of Weldon's test had stuck together. Weldon did not bother to check the numbers on the questions, so he missed two pages of questions. The way he finds out about that is that while he is discussing the questions, and answers with the other agents out in the hall, he discovers that some of those questions were not on his test. OOPS

We had been told at the beginning of the test that if that happened, if we skipped over some questions or we missed a page that would be just too bad. Now it has happened, and he is allowed to go back in and finish the test. Some agents are not too happy. They feel that he should have at least been given a different test since he had been discussing the answers with the other agents out in the hall. As it turns out, everyone passes the test. Of course, Weldon gets the highest score.

The Spanish exams will be Monday, April 21. We have heard some rumors that a hatchet man is being sent to give us our Spanish exams. We are also told that management wants to get rid of about five of us. The hatchet man is Chief Patrol Agent Bobby Rolls from McAllen, Texas. The second man giving the tests is Chief Patrol Agent Rolands; I haven't heard where he is from.

The first day of testing goes well, of four agents tested, everyone passed. The second day of testing, four agents are tested as well, but Frank Bigley fails. Everyone is shocked. How can that happen? Frank has never received less than eighty five percent on any test that he has taken so far, not even the surprise tests given at the academy. Frank didn't speak Spanish before coming into the Border Patrol, but he majored in English in college, so he has a very good background in language. He passed the five months Spanish exam with a score in the high eighties. The ten-month exam is exactly the same as the five-month exam. The degree of difficulty may be greater, but if so, not that much. There is a problem with Frank though, and that is his weight. Frank was about fifty pounds overweight when he went to the academy, but he has reduced about twenty five to thirty pounds since. Of course he is still a little heavy. Maybe the rumors are true.

The next day I'm off duty, but I hear through the grapevine that everyone has passed. I'm told that I will be the first one tested on the following day and that I should be there by 7:30 A.M.

I am there at 7:30, but Agent Jones tells me that they didn't get to test Chad Marley the day before, so I will have to wait until they finish testing him. About 9:00 A.M. Agent Jones comes back to the squad room where I'm waiting and tells me that the Chiefs have completed testing Marley and that he has failed.

Jones tells me I will be next after Tommy Newlin. I say, "I thought I was going to be next after Chad."

"Well, they didn't get to Tommy yesterday either, so they told him to come in at nine, and he would be tested second."

I say "OK." What can I say? They have all the cards. "Oh well, it all pays the same!" I sit back, and try to relax. It's not working. Have you ever had to wait outside the boss's office, knowing that when he calls you into his office, he is either going to fire you or promote you, depending on how well your interview goes? Well, that's how I'm feeling.

About 10:00 A.M. Doug Woolery and Pete Vinton show up. They are going to be the last two tested. The testing is supposed to be done alphabetically, so I expect to be next, then Woolery, then Vinton. At 10:30 Jones comes back and tells us that Newlin has passed, and the testers want Woolery next. Jones looks at me, and says, "I don't know what's going on I told them you were next, but they said, 'No, they want Woolery,' so that's what we have to do."

I cannot help thinking about that rumor. It is said that one of the agents in McAllen, Texas, overheard CPA Bobby Rolls say that he is going to El Paso to fire five trainees their names are Bigley, Marley, Woolery, Vinton, and Rambo. To this point Bigley and Marley have been fired; it doesn't look good.

It's noon, and here comes Jones again. They've finished testing Woolery, and he failed. Jones looks at me again, and I say, "Yeah, I know. They want Vinton next, and you don't know why."

"Right," he said.

About 1:15 Jones comes back to the squad room where I'm still waiting and tells me, "They've finished with Vinton, and it doesn't look like he's passed. He ran out of time and left several questions unanswered. He says he's pretty sure he didn't pass."

"So, do they want me now?"

"No, they say they're going to break for lunch. It'll be about an hour, or an hour and a half before they return."

"Damn, I guess I might as well get something to eat too."

I go down the street to a little hamburger joint and get myself a hamburger and fries and take them back to the station to eat. It's becoming funny. I'm sitting there with a big smile on my face, eating my hamburger, and trying to keep from laughing out loud when Bill Heyday walks in. Bill is one of the journeymen that I had worked with. Most trainees know him as "The hatchet man" because he loves to hand out some really bad appraisals. I get along with him just fine, but some of the guys have gotten some really bad reports from him. He asks me if I've been tested yet, and I shake my head no. He says, "You'll pass it there's not a doubt in my mind."

I say, "What do you know that no one else knows? It seems like everyone else knows that I'm going to fail".

"You know you're not," he says. "Look at yuh, sittin there eating your hamburger, almost laughing. You're the coolest son-of-a-bitch I've ever seen. They've been screwing with you all morning, and you're laughing at them. Actually they've been screwing with you since you first got here."

I say, "Well, maybe they've gone too far. Right now I don't much give a shit whether I pass or not. I'm not sure I even want to be in this outfit."

I finish my burger and fries, and I sit there for about another hour before the testers return from lunch. By now I'm thinking this whole fiasco is really hilarious. I'm also thinking, They might fire me, but by God they're going to correct every word on that test. I'm not going to leave anything blank. So far it seems like they've shook these guy's up so bad, that they don't even finish the test.

Finally Jones comes back and tells me they're ready for me. He says, "How are you holding up?"

"I'm just fine", I tell him. "If they're expecting a basket case to come walking in, they're going to be surprised".

Jones doesn't seem to hear that. He just goes to apologizing, "I'm really sorry. If I had known they weren't going to test you till the last, I wouldn't have had you come in till noon." I'm thinking, Yeah, right, Jones. I was born at night, but not last night. You've been planning this for weeks, maybe since the very beginning. I might be wrong about that, but I sure don't think so. I know that as for me and some of those others that have been fired, we didn't receive the instruction that we should have to pass the final exam.

Finally, here it is time to take the test. I'm ready for anything. I walk in, Jones introduces me to CPA Rolls and CPA Rolands, and then he leaves the room. Rolands will act as my alien. He explains, "The test will take one hour. When we begin the test, write the time we begin in the upper right corner of the test. Once the test has begun, everything will be conducted in Spanish. If you have any questions, you must ask them in Spanish. If you finish early and you wish to return to any portion of the test that you may have had trouble with, you must ask for that in Spanish. Any questions?"

"No Sir, I'm ready," I say. Everything about the test is exactly the same as the five month exam, except that the last twenty questions are more difficult. It is a smuggling case, but the questions are much more complex than on the five month exam.

Rolands says, "Begin". I write the time in the upper right corner of the exam paper, and I begin. I breeze right through the first twenty questions and the jurat. I check my watch when I finish the jurat; it has taken just twenty minutes. That leaves me forty minutes to complete the last twenty questions. I feel good about that.

The first two questions of the smuggling case are easy zip, zip, no problem. I'm about half way through the third question when my alien, CPA Rolands just pushes his chair back, gets up, and leaves the room. CPA Rolls has been sitting in the corner of the room at another desk, shuffling my C and E's (Journeyman evaluation papers), making as much noise as he can, in order to make sure I know exactly what he's doing. When Rolands leaves the room, Rolls continues to shuffle C and E's for a while. Finally he looks over at me, acts as if he's just figured out what's going on, gets up, comes over and sits down in front of me. He looks over the entire test, taking as much time as he can to figure out where I'm at, and then says, "Continue." I'm laughing. I mean right in the middle of this Dog and Pony Show, I start cracking up. I laugh out loud. I can't believe what these guy's are doing. They're openly trying to use up my time. I'm beginning to understand what happened to the others who failed. It seems as if five minutes have passed before I am able to continue, but in reality it might be only a minute and a half or so.

I continue, but I'm unable to ask the third question because I'm hung up on a noun. I ask to skip that question and go to the next. Maybe they've got me shook up, too. Then again, maybe I would have missed the word anyway I'll never know. I go to the next question.

Three questions later CPA Rolands comes back into the room. He and Rolls go through the entire Dog and Pony Show again, and it's still funny, I laugh. They waste another minute and a half of my time. I just can't believe it. I continue on, and although the questions are difficult, I don't get hung up on any of them.

Finally I reach the end of the exam. I look at my watch. There are five minutes remaining. In Spanish I ask to return to question number three. CPA Rolands says, "No, the test is over." I say, "No, I have five minutes remaining." He says, "No, Mr. Rambo, the test is over. You may leave the room while we check your test. We will call you back in when we are finished".

I record the time when he first told me that the test was over. I say "Thank you Sir," and I leave the room.

They have robbed me of 8 minutes of valuable testing time, but what can I do? I tell Jones and Simons what has happened just in case I have to do something about it later. Then I sit back and wait.

About 20 minutes later, they call me back into the room. I sit down at the desk, and CPA Rolands ask me, "How do you think you did?"

"I don't know how well I did." I say.

"You mean you don't know whether you passed the test or not?"

"Oh yes! I passed the test; I just don't know what score I'm getting," I say.

"Well, you're right. You did pass the test. You got 73.8%. Is that what you expected?"

"It's good enough for me," I said. Seventy-three percent or a hundred percent, it all pays the same. They both shake my hand, and I leave the room. I pass the test, but none of us make any friends that day.

All of us trainees are planning to celebrate after the testing is finished, but because so many fail we change our minds. It just doesn't really feel like a joyful occasion. I ask several people, but nobody seems to be in the party mood, so Jackie and I go out to dinner by ourselves. I am, after all, very happy to still be employed.

CHAPTER 9

The Sheriff of Pecos County

It's the first of May, and we're real busy in the Border Patrol. It is always busy at this time of the year. I'm working the four to midnight shift at the head-gate area with my partner, Terry Pallaqi. Terry's a big man, about six foot, three inches tall, and he weighs about two hundred and ten pounds. Terry's most outstanding feature is his long, long arms. Everyone teases Terry about making four tracks in the sand when he walks through the desert.

He's very fit and enjoys taking trainees just back from the Academy up Mount Cristo Rey. He will tell them that Border Bandits hang out at the top of the mountain and rob tourists from both sides of the border when they go up to visit the statute of Jesus on the Cross. Then he tells them that they need to go up and check it out. Of course, that's all true, but that's not the real reason Terry wants to go to the top of the mountain. Terry wants to show the trainees that even though they have just completed a rigorous course of training at the Academy, they're still no match for him when it comes to climbing mountains.

Terry tries to pull that one on me. What Terry doesn't know is I was climbing mountains for a living before I came to the Academy, and the mountains that I was climbing make Mt. Cristo Rey look like a sand dune. When we start up the mountain, I soon take the lead, and after going about 300 yards, I'm about 100 yards ahead. Terry yells up to me, and says, "That's far enough, we can see enough from here." I figured that game out real fast.

I like Terry, and that's a good thing because we're in the same unit, and I will be working with him a lot. Unit 4 is a real good unit, and I like everyone in this unit, including our supervisor, John O'Neall. Mr. O'Neall, or Boss, which is what everyone calls him, is half Cherokee Indian. He doesn't look Indian. He is fair complexioned and bald, but he sure knows how to follow tracks like an Indian. He likes to catch snakes, and he always keeps a few around the house. Snakes are the reason he's missing the end of the little finger on his left hand. One bit him while he was handling them.

It's been a beautiful day and even a more beautiful evening and night. We're having a full moon, and it's almost as bright as day. Almost as bright as day, that is, everywhere except around the Asarco copper refining plant, where the smoke is nearly blocking out the moon completely. Asarco is just a short distance west of our position, and we're getting plenty of smoke also.

Asarco and the EPA seemed to have some sort of agreement going. During the day there doesn't seem to be any smoke coming from the big smokestack or anywhere else on the plant. When the sun goes down though, and I mean the minute the sun goes down, smoke starts pouring out of the top of the smokestack and out of the bottom of the smokestack, and it appears to be coming out of every building on the plant site. When the sun comes up in the morning, the smoke will be shut off completely again. The people of El Paso get up in the morning, look out their windows, see all the smoke, and blame it on the Mexicans. They never question Asarco or the EPA because you can see there isn't any smoke coming from the Asarco Plant.

After working a night shift down around Asarco, I cough up black tar for a couple of days.

Bud Dunham and his partner, Don Hart, are working the area west of the head gates. They're parked in an area of the Asarco Plant that overlooks the river. At about five minutes to midnight, Bud calls and tells us that he and Don are watching some activity in the river below. He says it looks like there are four people coming across the river. He wants to know if we will be available to cut off their retreat back into Mexico once they have come far enough into the U.S., to allow us to do that.

Terry tells him, "Sure, just let us know when they get far enough in."

About five minutes later Bud calls, "They've crossed Paisano Street, and they're on the railroad tracks at this time, so come on in and block them off".

"OK, we're on the way." We head west on Paisano. It's only about a half mile from our position, and so I guess that it took less than a minute to get there. Even so, Dunham, and Hart already have the four in custody, so we continue on up into the plant where they have their car parked.

When we arrive, we're a little surprised to see two gringos and two Mexicans. It's very rare to find gringos smuggling Mexicans unless it's a housewife smuggling her maid. It is very rare for gringos to be smuggling any people. They may be a part of the operation or the head of the operation, but they are rarely found crossing the river with the aliens. The most surprising thing though is the sheriff's badge on the tall gringo with the hat, and the sheriff's deputy badge on the other gringo. The Sheriff claims to be from Pecos County. The Mexicans are wearing handcuffs and according to the Sheriff, are his prisoners.

Bud and Don do most of the questioning, because they are the arresting officers. Terry and I are just helping them.

Bud asks, "Why are these prisoners wanted?"

The Sheriff introduces himself as Sheriff Grimes, and says, "Well, these boys is witness to a murder over in Pecos County. We're jes gonna take em back over to Fort Stockton and have em testify; then we're gonna bring em back."

Bud says, "Sheriff, I'm sure you realize that Juarez is in Mexico, and that Mexico is not a part of the United States, so therefore you do not have authority to arrest anyone over there."

"Well, yeah, I guess that's technically correct, but they're not really under arrest, just temporarily restrained."

Bud says, “Yeah, right. Get in the back, and let’s go to the office. You guys take the Mexicans in your car, so we can keep them separate.”

“Right, we’ve got them," Terry says. It’s quitting time, so we take them to Sector Headquarters, where there will be less turmoil.

When we arrive at Sector, we keep everyone separate, and Bud starts making phone calls. Terry and I start talking to the Mexicans. What we discover by talking to the Mexicans is that their stories about the murder don’t match. In fact, they’re so vague about the murder that both Terry and I come to the same conclusion at the same time. They didn’t see any murder at all.

Bud is still on the phone, and Don is still talking to the Deputy. Terry and I sort of listen in on Don and the deputy for a few minutes, and after listening, decide the deputy doesn’t know much more about this murder than the Mexicans do. Finally Bud gets off the phone, comes over to where we are, and tells us what he’s found out. He says he called the sheriff's office in Fort Stockton and talked to the deputy that’s been left in charge. He says the deputy is unaware of any murder trial taking place in Pecos County at this time or at any other time in the near future. He also tells Bud that he has no idea that the Sheriff is out of town. He says he’s sure the Sheriff is out at his ranch.

So the Sheriff has a ranch. Bud gets the phone number from the deputy and calls the ranch. The lady that answers the phone tells Bud that the sheriff has gone to

El Paso. She will not tell him why he went to El Paso but says he should be home early in the morning and that Bud should call back then. She won't tell him who she is either, but he figures she's the wife of the sheriff. We already know why he's in El Paso. He's in El Paso so he can cross the border into Juarez, Mexico, and pick up his hired hands. Now all we have to do is get a confession.

After hearing everything that Bud has to tell us, Terry and I go back to talk to the Mexicans. The guy I'm talking to is Jose Manuel Torres Soledad. I say, "Jose, we already know that you and your friend are going to work on the sheriff's ranch. We know there wasn't a murder committed and that therefore you are not witnesses. Jose, would you like to tell me the real truth?"

"Si, Senor. Yo he trabajado por el senor Grimes por como cinco anos, mas o menos. Como dos semanas antes La Migra vengan al rancho del Senor Grimes, y me arrestado." (Translation: "Yes, Sir. I have worked for Mr. Grimes for about five years, more or less. About two weeks ago the Border Patrol came to Mr. Grime's ranch, and arrested me.")

"Was your friend Francisco working there also?"

"Yes, Sir."

"Will you say this when you go before the judge?"

"Yes, Sir."

I go over and talked to Bud again.

"Jose tells me that he and Francisco have been working for the Sheriff for about five years, and about two weeks ago the Border Patrol arrested them and sent them back to Mexico."

"Is that right? Well, let me talk to the sheriff again." Bud goes back to interrogate the sheriff again. About ten minutes pass. Bud comes back and says, "Well, the Sheriff has confessed to smuggling the two Mexicans, so let's write them up".

"Oh, by the way, the Deputy is not a Deputy. He is the ranch foreman".

We write them up and go home. A couple of days later, we all go to court. The judge listens to the testimony and finds in favor of the prosecution. The sheriff and his foreman are both found guilty of two counts of alien smuggling. The judge sentences the sheriff to two years probation and a $50.00 fine for each alien. The foreman is given one year's probation, and no fine.

As we walk out of the courtroom Terry looks at the rest of us and says, "Now isn't that a kick-in-the-ass? The judge says, 'Give me a hundred dollars and don't do that again for two years'."

Don says, "Yeah, I guess the sheriff has already told them that they will have to get to the ranch on their own 'cause he's not going to be able to pick 'em up this time."

CHAPTER 10

The Hole in One Boys

The Border Patrol, like most law enforcement agencies works around the clock. Generally a twenty four hour period consists of three shifts: the day shift (8:00 A.M. to 4:00 P.M.), the swing shift (4:00 P.M. to 12:00 A.M.), and the graveyard shift (12:00 A.M. to 8:00 A.M.). We rotate shifts every two weeks, two weeks on days, two weeks on swing, and two weeks on graveyard. The pay period is also two weeks, so we rotate every pay period. My unit is on the graveyard shift this pay period. The graveyard shift is aptly named because nothing seems to be moving; the city becomes a graveyard. You'd think that because there isn't much going on at that time of night, it would be easier to work. For many people it is, though for the majority it isn't because it just isn't natural to be up at that time of night. If God wanted us to work through the night, He would have given us eyes that could see in the dark.

Although sleeping while on duty is a firing offense, I will venture to say that probably everyone that has ever worked a midnight to eight shift has dozed off at least a time or two. Even though my sciatic nerve acts up after sitting still in a car seat for just a short time, I still manage to doze off now and then.

Unit Four has been on graveyard shift for a little over a week now, and everyone seems a little zombie like.

I'm assigned to work the Second Street area with Ronnie Crane.

Ronnie is a funny guy. One time we were having a Unit meeting, and Leonard Walden was complaining about the way we work the airport. He thinks we should work it more like the Marine Corps would work it. Len is an ex-Marine and thinks everything we do should be done like the Marines. He says he thinks we should be assigned specific areas of the airport, and along with that we should have some training to work those areas. It's his opinion that by the time we get into the swing of things and learn how to work the airport, our shift at the airport is over. Ronnie looks over at Len and says, "Yeah, right, Len-the El Paso Airport is so huge, it must take all of ten minutes to figure out how to work it." He has a very dry sense of humor.

Ronnie came into the Border Patrol when he was about 23 or 24 years old. I didn't come in until I was almost 36, so he's quite a bit younger than I am, but he has been in the patrol about a year longer than I have.

We check out a couple of hand-held radios and go looking for our car. After we've located our car and determined that it doesn't have any new dents or scratches, we head for the Kettle to get a cup of coffee.

Lonnie Norman and Don Jensen are parking their car in front of the Kettle just as we arrive. We walk in and sit with Lonnie and Don at a booth by the window. We all order a piece of pie and a cup of coffee. Just as the waitress turns to go, Lonnie cancels his pie order. He always does that. Lonnie has a weight problem and wages a constant battle with his appetite. He always loses the battle, but he has to do battle to ease his conscience. For instance, I know from experience that he will cancel that pie order, but as soon as he leaves the Kettle he will head straight for Church's Chicken and order three pieces of white meat, an order of fries, and a large Coke. In fact, he might not be able to go without the pie.

Lonnie is a very good friend of mine. He's African-American, a little overweight, and a really nice guy. OK! He's a lot overweight. Like me, Lonnie didn't come into the Border Patrol until he was about thirty five or thirty six years old. Lonnie has been with the U.S. Government most of his life though. He was a Postal Worker for about fourteen years.

Now Don, on the other hand, is grossly overweight, but he isn't even pretending to diet. Don is a middle-aged white guy and a real slob. Don will order two or three Burritos; lie back in his car seat, and let the grease run down the front of his shirt. He doesn't even attempt to clean it up. It's real embarrassing to work with Don. Aside from that, Don is a pretty nice guy. Something surprising about Don though is he always has two or three young girls chasing after him. I've never been able to figure out what the attraction is. Of course, I haven't tried very hard.

The waitress comes over to refill our coffee cups. Lonnie says, "Miss, I've changed my mind. I believe I will have a piece of that chocolate pie".

Lonnie has a story he likes to tell on himself about the Academy. When Lonnie's class was at the Academy, they were sent back to their duty stations for a month or two because illegal aliens were inundating the U.S. at an unprecedented rate. If I remember correctly, this call back was named Operation Hold the Line. The way Lonnie tells it, when he was at the Academy for the first half of his training, he would get so horny he could hardly stand it. Whenever this would happen, he would take out Ole Black Magic, which is what he calls his male member, and slam it in the door. According to Lonnie, the door was getting quite a work-out. When he returned to the Academy for the second half of his training, they assigned him to a different room. He said he was heart-broken, for he had fallen in love with the door on his first room. He said he never fully recovered.

It's 1:00 A.M. by the time we get down to the river. Ronnie and I are assigned the Second Street to Chamizal Bridge area. Lonnie and Don are assigned the area from Chamizal to Val Verde Street, which is right next to us. We are fairly busy for about an hour after we get to the river; then things get really quiet. It's hard to work the Chamizal area at this time because the highway department is constructing a new interchange right at the bridge. In another way, though, the construction makes it easier because there are built up areas where you can park and see for a long distance. Lonnie and Don have staked out this high ground for themselves. From there they can see all the way down the Border Highway to Val Verde Street.

It's quiet, real quiet. Ronnie and I sit and talk for a long time; then we both get quiet. I'm thinking that I haven't even heard the dispatcher for at least two hours, and he's supposed to do a security check every hour. He must be asleep, too.

All at once the radio goes off like a shotgun in the middle of the night. I must have dozed off. Ronnie and I both bolt upright in the seat look all around, eyes wide open. If anyone's watching us, they probably think we're under attack.

The dispatcher is saying, "I have a report of twenty aliens running across the Border Highway about a quarter of a mile east of the Chamizal Bridge".

Lonnie answers, "Ten Four, Ten Four, we've got em in sight, and we're on our way".

Just the way he answers, you can tell he just woke up, just like us and probably everyone else on the river. Ronnie and I both look over at the Chamizal Bridge area at the same time. We don't see any sign of Lonnie and Don. We look at each other, and Ronnie says, "Man, they're quick". I say, "Yep, I guess we should go help them".

We start in that direction and try to call them, but someone seems to have a stuck mike button. All we can hear is a loud, shhhhhhhhhhhhhhhhhhhhhhhhhhhhhhh hh hhhhhhhhhhhhhhhhhhhhhhhhhh. We continue east and eventually find the aliens. There aren't twenty of them, but there are about fifteen. Finally the radio clears up, and we're able to talk. We call Lonnie and Don. We don't get an answer. We call again. Still no answer. We need help to transport these people, but we aren't able to get Lonnie and Don, so we call for a D.O. (Detention Officer). As soon as we call for the D.O., the stuck mike starts again. Shhhhhhhhhhhhhhh hhhhhhhhhhhhhhhhhhhhhhhhhhhhh.

This stuck mike is really getting old. Finally the D.O. shows up, and we load up the people. We tell him to keep them separate, and we will be in to write them up as soon as we're able to locate Lonnie and Don. We search and search, but we are unable to locate them. We can't get in touch with them on the radio because of that damned stuck mike. We know they're out there somewhere looking for those aliens because they're no longer up on the high ground where they were.

Finally we go into the PDN to write up the aliens. Most of them have already been written up by the time we get there because everyone is so bored out on the line that they come in and help us. Everyone that is, but Lonnie and Don. Still we have to listen to that damned stuck mike.

Ronnie and I go back out to look some more. We decide to park up on the spot where Lonnie and Don were parked, and maybe we will be able to see them from there. As we get closer to the high ground we can see what appears to be a light shining in the air. We drive on up to where the light is shining in the air, and what do you suppose we find? There are several holes drilled in the ground for pilings to support the overpass that is being built. These are going to be very large pilings. They need very large holes to accept the very large pilings. The holes are also big enough to accept a rather small Jeep Comanche, which is what Lonnie and Don are driving.

It isn't hard to figure out what happened. When they got the call, they were both asleep. Lonnie just threw that Jeep in reverse, and without thinking, backed right into one of those big holes. The hole was so tight; they couldn't even open a door. Because VHF Radios are line-of-sight transmission and they are below ground, the guys can't even call for help. All they can do is key the mike and hope someone will get mad enough to come looking for them.

There is no way for us to pull them out of that hole. The only way they are ever coming up out of that hole is to be lifted straight up. That will require a big wrecker or a crane. We decide to try the wrecker first. In the meantime Lonnie and Don just have to sit there and gaze at the stars and try to come up with a very good memo to explain this situation.

About 30 minutes later the wrecker shows up. Of course, the wrecker doesn't get there as fast as the entire midnight shift. There were about ten guys wearing green uniforms staring down into those star-gazing faces at least ten minutes before the wrecker showed up. The wrecker driver hooks the cable up to the frame and inches them up out of the hole. They are very happy to be on solid, flat ground and to be able to open their doors. Of course, they are also very embarrassed.

Forever after, they will be known as The Hole in One Boys.

CHAPTER 11

The Spook

It seems like I usually have a good time when I work the sand-hills. I don't know why maybe it's the freedom that the area affords.

Working the sand-hills consists of searching the desert that surrounds the El Paso area for aliens or sign of aliens that have crossed the border into the United States. This activity is also known as sign cutting. The Border Patrol has always, as far as I know, maintained a drag road parallel to the border. First, a drag road is created by using a bulldozer or a road grader to make a level, passable road. Then old tires, heavy timber, or iron rails, (something heavy) will be dragged along that road periodically to wipe out any old sign that might be there. It's kind of like smoothing out the sand in a sand box. That way if anyone crosses the trail, it will be readily apparent. This activity is usually done daily. Checking for new sign is also done on a regular basis, at least once daily. The agent drives beside the drag trail with a sedan, a 4-wheel drive vehicle, an airplane, or helicopter, looking for fresh footprints in the smoothed out sand.

We also have sensor devices implanted in various places along the border where people tend to cross most frequently. Some of the devices detect footsteps, some detect movement, and some detect heat, etc... Some of these sensors are more reliable than others. For instance, if you have a foot sensor in an area where there are a lot of animals, animals frequently set it off. When the agent arrives and does not find any people or any sign of people, he will often become discouraged even though he knows that it was probably animals that set it off. The next time the sensor goes off he may not be so quick to respond, thinking that it is probably animals again. For that reason, the sensor implant people usually research the area very well to determine what sensor will get the best response.

These devices are monitored at a central location, and when they are tripped, the number representing that sensor is called out on the radio. The person nearest to the location will respond. Generally that will be the person assigned to that location, but if that person is unavailable, the next closest person will respond.

I hope this explanation will give you a general idea of how the Border Patrol works the sand hills. Of course, some areas are easier and more fun to work than others. One of those fun places is located in the Anapra area, just west of El Paso.

In the Anapra area the Rio Grande River is not the established border between Mexico and the United States. The river becomes the border about a mile and a half east of that area.

This trail runs right along the Southern bank of the Rio Grande River, and in some areas it's very sandy. We've implanted a sensor in the trail where it is almost impossible to avoid. To get around it is very difficult. Further up-stream, in a spot that takes approximately twenty minutes at a brisk walk to reach, is located a small, but very sandy hill that the trail goes over. In order to climb this little hill, it's almost always necessary to get down on all fours and crawl over it, especially if it's really dry and the sand is especially loose. When a group is involved, this causes quite a commotion.

There are a number of interesting apprehensions that have taken place in this area. One that I will never forget happened on Halloween night of 1978.

That day I notice as we leave Station One that my partner, Robert Guerra, has picked up a old mask that has been lying around the station for a couple of weeks. I guess one of the aliens brought it in when he was arrested and just left it there. It's one of those masks that has a knife slash across a large, ugly, twisted face. Many of the teeth are missing, and one eye is missing. It's a hideous looking thing.

Early in the evening we respond to the above mentioned sensor, but because we we're so close when the sensor goes off, we don't wait for the people to reach the area that I just described. Instead we choose a spot about half way and wait for whoever or whatever is coming down the trail. It turns out to be just one guy. We arrest him, and we're headed back to our vehicle, when my partner spots an old, black, trench coat that's lying on the trail. It has been there for days, and no one has paid any attention to it until now. Robert picks it up, dusts it off and carries it back to the vehicle. I can't figure out why he wants this old dirty trench coat, but a lot of what Robert does doesn't make sense to me. I'm sure he's planning something, and I figure I will find out what it is sooner or later.

It's getting close to midnight, about 11:15 or 11:30, I'd guess, when we receive a call from Radio. The sensor down on the river has just gone off again. The radio operator says it looks like about ten to fifteen aliens. He can tell that by the amount of times and the frequency that the sensor goes off.

We're close to the area, so we have plenty of time to set up. When we reach the area, I take the north side of the trail, and Robert takes the south side. There isn't even a sliver of moon tonight, so it's very dark. We're only about fifteen feet apart, and we can't even see each other's outline. We remain completely quiet for about ten or fifteen minutes.

The aliens are being very quiet also, but we're still able to hear them from about twenty yards away. We can hear them as they start up the little sand hill. They're not being quiet now. They're clawing to get up the hill. We can't see them, but we can tell where they are by the sounds. As each one reaches the top, he stops to wait for the others.

Just as the last one reaches the top, I hear a loud grunting and then a roaring noise. At first I thought it was a bear, but then an ugly head appears, and it seems to be floating in thin air. It is illuminated as if it is creating it's own light. It's very scary, and I almost run.

Then the damnedest commotion you've ever heard breaks out. I'm afraid I'm going to get run over. I turn on my flashlight and yell, "Parase" (which means stop in Spanish). I shine my light all around the perimeter; there isn't anyone there except my silly looking partner.

There he stands with that damned black trench coat on, buttoned all the way up to his neck, one hand inside the coat with his little penlight sticking out just below the chin of that ugly mask. It was an eerie sight, out there in the middle of nowhere in the pitch-black night. I make one more pass with my light.

My God, what a sight! There on top of a wobbly wooden fence post is perched a little gray headed guy. He has both feet on top of the post just like a bird. The guy is only about 5 feet tall, and he's probably 50 years old. He's shaking like a leaf. I mean shaking violently, like he's scared half to death. How the hell did he get up there? I know you can do a lot of things if you're scared enough, but I don't think you can fly.

Robert is still standing there laughing like a crazy man. I start to chew him out for scaring this man half to death, but it is really funny. Besides, anyone that could stand on a fence post like that is a long way from being dead.

After we pull ourselves together, we decide to see if we can find any of the others. We shine our lights all around on the tracks. From the looks of those tracks, it's amazing that nobody has been trampled to death. We try, but we never find any of the others. It's just as well; they probably wouldn't have been able to talk either. The one we have doesn’t even know his own name.

CHAPTER 12

Potluck Parson

There are a lot of people milling around in the squad
room. It is about 4:00 P.M. and some agents are coming off the day shift while others are waiting for muster to begin for the evening shift. There is also a smuggling case from El Salvador that is being processed. All the restrooms are being used in the squad room, so the only ones available are the executive rest rooms. That's what we call the rest rooms up front that the chief, assistant chiefs, and visitors use. So when Potluck Parson has to relieve himself that's where he goes. Potluck is assigned to the desk because of something he said about the Chief. I've never been able to find out what he said.

Potluck is pretty verbal. I remember this happening one day when I was working the desk, and all the others were doing there daily activity reports. This middle aged couple came into the squad room, and the lady walks over to the desk and said to me, "We have a son in the Border Patrol, and he is stationed in San Diego, California. We were just curious about what Border Patrol Agents do".

Potluck hadn't seemed to even notice the couple when they walked in, and without looking up from his paperwork, he says, using his best Charlie Chapman impression, which by the way is pretty good, "Lady, I would rather have my daughter in a whore-house, than have my son in the Border Patrol." The lady just turned around and walked out, her husband close behind.

While Potluck is relieving himself on this day, one of the other agents walks in and says, "I understand you're working the desk because of what you said about the Chief." Potluck looks at the guy and says, "Some-body ought to kill that son-of-a-bitch, and maybe I'll just do that some day." They both zip up and walk out, never noticing the pair of boots showing under the door in one of the stalls. Those boots belong to Chief Nelson.

The next day Potluck is not just working the desk. He is assigned to the desk until further notice. He is also relieved of his gun and badge until further notice.

I don't know how Mr. Parson ever got the name Potluck, and I guess I never will, but I know that almost every other agent in the El Paso Station seems to have a nick name, and Potluck Parson is the one that handed out most of those nick-names. For instance, Chainsaw Walden is so named because he snores so loud it sounds like a chainsaw. Smokestack Hollis is named because of his constant smoking. Dog Dodson got his name because he spends his spare time and who knows what other time calling in coyotes so that he can kill them. Texas Tim Johnson got his name by being thoroughly Texas. The Golden Boy Daniels is named because he has golden hair and seems to always be in the right place at the right time, especially for promotions.

Of course, Potluck is always there to get a trainee started off on the right foot. He always explains the job in the same manner: big cases-big problems; little cases-little problems; no cases-no problems.

Right now though, Potluck isn't very happy. He still rails against the Chief, but he does not like working the desk, (nobody does), and he desperately wants back in the field. He wants back so badly that finally he cools it enough to get the Chief to set him free.

One day not too long after that incident is over, Chief Nelson comes wandering back into the squad room, drifts on over to the supervisors office, and goes in. Walters is the only supervisor in at the time. He says, "Hi, Chief". I can hear him, not very well, but I can hear him.

Nelson doesn't return the greeting. He has a big grin on his face, and he says, "Walters, is it true that Potluck calls you Boliver Keg Ass".

Walters is about 50 pounds overweight. He looks up, smiles and says, "Yeah, and he calls you Shithouse Slim". Now that remark comes as a complete surprise; the look on Nelson's face is priceless. He makes a little choking sound, and leaves the room.

CHAPTER 13

The Great Tug of War on the Rio Grande

Here I am back on midnight shift again, and I'm working with Don Hart. I don't mind midnights this time because it is mid summer, 1979, and the days are hotter than Hades.

Don and I have a few things in common, so we get along pretty well. We're both about the same size, we enjoy each other's dry sense of humor, and we're both pilots. I haven't landed on the Ft. Bliss Golf Course yet like Don has, but if Don had had just one more gallon of gasoline, he probably wouldn't have landed there either because he would have made it to the El Paso Airport. The Ft. Bliss Golf Course is located about two miles northeast of the El Paso Airport. When the engine on his Cessna 150 died, Bill was real happy to have any place to land, even if it was a golf course. On the other hand though, it was very embarrassing. He had all those golfers teasing him about putting his airplane in the rough. Every one of the BP agents that found out about it had something to say. Such as, "If you're going to fly an airplane, you should put in more than five dollars worth of gas at a time." "Did you really run out of gas, or did someone knock your little airplane out of the sky with a golf ball?" "If you can't tell the difference between a golf course and an airport, do you really think you should be flying?" "Airports are the ones with the long black fairways." Don takes it all in good humor.

Don and I have been assigned to the same unit for about a year now and we work together quite a lot. For the past couple of months we've been working city patrol. During the day we usually work construction sites; four to midnight we work the bars, and there isn't any midnight shift on city patrol.

We usually work together as a unit on city patrol. The reason for this is that while working construction we need to have as many agents as are available to chase the aliens that run in every direction as soon as they spot our vehicles. When we work the bars, we need as many agents as possible for security reasons. The patrons are usually drunk, and they become very unruly when we take the ladies (topless dancers, barmaids, etc.) from them. We've learned with experience that the trouble always starts with the little guys going after the biggest agents they can find. It seems as if they get real macho after a couple of drinks, and they have to prove how tough they are. Once we figure this out, we decide that a couple of us agents that aren't quite so intimidating should go in by ourselves. Don and I are usually among the ones to go in. We identify ourselves and joke around a little with the patrons while we check everyone in the bar, whether they look illegal or not. We don't want to be accused of discriminating against anyone. Whenever we find someone that's illegal, we simply tell him or her to go outside where the other agents are waiting. It works very well. If we do have any trouble, we can always call the other agents. You know what-we never did have to call on the other agents.

In the past the Border Patrol never did anything with these girls, except to put them back across the border. Whenever we went back to a bar, after having checked it previously, we would almost always find the same girls working the same job.

A couple of weeks ago the Border Patrol changed their policy. The new policy is that any barmaids or topless dancers that we arrest three times or more will go to jail. The normal sentence is a year. They will probably only serve three to six months, but it is a very good deterrent.

One day while working construction, Don and I answer a call from the dispatcher. He asks us to go to an apartment complex and talk to the woman at the office. He says she is reporting several illegal aliens living in one room. We go to the complex, and the woman points out the room where the aliens are living.

We don't have a search warrant, but we decide to go up and knock on the door anyway. A girl answers the door, and I ask her citizenship. Before she even answers, I recognize her; she's one of the topless dancers that we've already arrested twice before. One of the reasons I recognize her is she's topless. Another reason is that she is Negrita, which in Spanish means that she is part Negro. She is also very, very pretty. That's all we need - we have to go in with her to make sure she doesn't escape. When we get inside, we find a group of at least ten female dancers. Some are completely dressed, but most are in various stages of undress. Here we have many of the female dancers that we have arrested in various nightclubs all over the city for the past two months all in one room. Most of them have already been arrested at least twice, so they are probably going to jail. Most of them are very pretty girls, and two of them are beautiful enough to be models. One of those is the Negrita.

That all happened on city patrol, and now here we are on midnight line watch. Nothing has happened so far, and it is real boring. Don and I are assigned the Head-gates area, which consists of everything west from about midway between the West Railroad Bridge and the head-gates to the Brick plant Bridge. It is about 4:30 A.M., and we're just driving past the head-gates. The head-gates are closed completely, diverting all of the water from the Rio Grande River into the irrigation canal system, so the river east of the head-gates is dry. There isn't any water running in the Rio Grande River east of the head-gates. The riverbed is still muddy though because the water has just been shut off a few hours ago.

Don and I both do a double take when we see the Ford Bronco stuck in the middle of the river. We look at each other in disbelief. That Bronco, because it is so heavily loaded, is up to the running boards in mud. We both know what that means. Drugs. Don reaches for the mike and calls the dispatcher. He tells her, "Send a wrecker, and tell him to get here as fast as possible".

I say, “You better have her call Customs while she’s at it; you know there is weed in that Bronco."

Don says, “Right, and I’ll bet a Mexican wrecker shows up here before very long."

We walk down to the river and examine the Bronco. Sure enough, it's loaded with marijuana. We get a license plate number and go back to our vehicle. When we get back to the car, we run a check on the license plate, and as we expect, it comes back as a stolen vehicle.

"Oh, oh! Here comes that Mexican wrecker."

"Yeah, but here comes our wrecker too." They both show up at the same time. Both wrecker drivers are hooking their cables up to the Bronco at the same time.

Then the Judiciales (Mexican Federal Police) show up. They jump out of their vehicle, draw their weapons, and point them at us. We get behind our vehicle, draw our weapons, and point them at the judiciales. Here comes a Huey helicopter. It's a Customs helicopter, the side door is open, and a Customs Agent with an M-16 rifle is hanging out the door. So now we have Judiciales pointing weapons at us and the helicopter, the customs agents and us pointing our weapons at them. It seems like we have a Mexican standoff.

The wreckers are going back and forth, back and forth. One gets a little better footing, and then the other gets a little better footing. This might go on forever.

"We don't want to see who runs out of gas first, do we Don?" I say, "I think we better call for the big wrecker, the one they use to pull out the big tractor trailer rigs." We do, and it shows up surprisingly fast.

When it gets here, the driver hooks up to the front of the American wrecker, and starts pulling everything across the river, the Bronco, the Mexican wrecker, everything. The guy with the Mexican wrecker really starts scrambling. He releases the cable, runs around to the back of the Bronco and unhooks the cable as fast as he can. Lucky for him he's fast enough; otherwise, he would be in the United States too. The judiciales are not ready to give up, but they have to because they have already lost their load. They do not want to start a war with the United States, but that load belongs to them. I mean literally that load belongs to the Mexican Judiciales. We drew our weapons in self-defense, but they did not. They drew their weapons and pointed them at us without provocation.

The best part of this operation is that we don't have much paper work to do. All we have to do is fill out an I-44, and turn it over to customs. Customs will take <u>all</u> the credit of course.

For at least a week we can't go into a restaurant or anywhere else in El Paso without hearing about the great tug-of-war down on the Rio Grande.

CHAPTER 14

The Patriot

It's a balmy Sunday morning in the latter part of April, 1980. I'm working the West Railroad Bridge. As I explained before, there are two ways to work the bridge either back off and let the aliens in or plug the hole. I am plugging the hole.

I'm sitting in my cruiser at the very end of Chihuahua Street. There is a small tree on the east side of the street. It doesn't give off much shade, but that's all there is, so here I sit. I have all the windows and the driver's side door open, so there is a nice, pleasant, little breeze flowing though the car. I've got the Sunday edition of the El Paso Times scattered all over the front seat of the car. I'm in the process of reading every word in that newspaper.

The only problem with these beautiful spring days is that everyone wants to go some place. A horde of Mexicans are hoping to go to the United States on this day. There are at least three hundred of them on, around, and under the West Bridge that would like to go to the U.S. They are also lined up along the rail at the top of the riverbank, on both sides of the river, from the bridge all the way to the old pump house. The old pump house is about a hundred and fifty yards west of the bridge, and the Mexicans use it as their toilet house. The new pump house is located directly north of the bridge, on the north side of the levee road, which runs directly between the pump house and the bridge. The new pump house is also directly between the bridge and me. Therefore, the people on the bridge are unable to see me, and I'm unable to see them. I like it that way, because it's less intimidating.

It's not impossible to get by me. I know that, and every one of the little river rats (homeless kids that live on the river) know that. They know that if two or more of them work together, they can get around me. All they have to do is go around both sides of me at the same time, and one side will make it through. I know that and they know that, but those other people up on the bridge don't know that. So I just let the kids go around both sides of me and let those other people think it's kid's day. Those kids aren't going anywhere anyway.

Speaking of those homeless kids, there are thousands of them all along the U.S./Mexican Border. We see them as dirty little urchins that hang around the downtown areas on both sides of the border. They're beggars, thieves, and in general, a big nuisance. Most range in age from four or five years old, to twenty years old. I, for one, admire those kids. Left on their own they have no one to take care of them. With no home, no food and no clothes provided for them they still manage to survive. They make it solely by their wits, and they do it in good humor. When it snows they go look for a Border Patrol Agent to arrest them, so they can go to jail and warm up. Most of the time, though, they live out in the weather with whatever nature hands them, these kids are very tough. Many of them eventually turn to drugs to ease their pain. The drugs they normally turn to are glue and paint, usually silver paint because they say it works better.

Many of them don't live past twenty five or thirty years of age. We criticize them, but they are just trying to cope.

I came on duty at 8:00 A.M., and arrived at the bridge about 8:30 A.M. We have been playing the game for about three hours now, so I guess it's about 11:30 or 12:00. I hear a noise, a vehicle coming up the street very fast. I look in the rear view mirror. I'm both startled and amused by what I see. There is a Ford pick-up truck speeding up behind me.

I'll try to describe the truck, but I doubt if I can do it justice. It is a real work of art. First of all, it's about a 1953 or 54 model Ford, the kind that has the fenders molded around the wheels, front and back with a running board in between. It's red, white, and blue. It has four American Flags: two at the front of the front fenders, and two at the front of the cab. The flags are about ten inches wide and eighteen inches long. It has red, white, and blue mud flaps all around and it has Mexican license plates. What a sight.

The truck slides to a stop, with tires squealing, about two feet away from my cruiser. Now I can see the driver. He belongs with the truck. He's a piece of work. He appears to be sitting on a pillow or something. I don't think he's very tall, because he has real short arms. He is very stocky however, not fat. He has one muscular arm hanging out the window; the other one is gripping the steering wheel. He's Mexican. He has a black eye, and he's wearing a headband. Red, white, and blue, of course.

He says, “Hey Meester, jew nid sum hep?"

“No, I’m doing fine. Thanks anyway,” I say. I am trying very hard not to laugh.

“Well, Meester, I’m seeing all dem Mexicans ober der, an eet lukes lak jew needs sum hep, an I wants to hep jew. Let me haf jor pistola meester, and I weel take care uf dem."

“No, I can’t let you have my gun.”

“O.K. Meester, let me hab jor steek."

“No, I can’t do that either."

“O.K. Meester, I weel chust haf to jews my belt,”

With that he jumps out of his pick-up truck, jerks off his belt, and starts running toward the bridge swinging the belt over his head. I'm thinking, man this guy’s going to get himself killed, but I'm laughing so hard I can't do anything about it. Anyway, he's obviously on a mission. It's the funniest sight I've seen in a long time. Picture this! This guy is just slightly over five feet tall and weighs about two hundred pounds. He has real short legs, and when he runs, he looks like a bear trying to run on his hind legs. In addition to that, he’s holding his pants up with one hand and swinging the belt with the other.

He disappears around the corner of the new pump house. For about thirty seconds, maybe less, I can’t see him or hear him. I'm beginning to worry. If something happens to this guy I might have a hard time explaining why I allowed this to happen. Soon everything goes completely quiet, and I'm beginning to imagine him lying there with his throat cut.

All at once a tremendous cheer goes up. It's a cheer like you might expect to hear at a football stadium when the home team has scored. I'm thinking. Oh my God, they've killed him. Then he appears, running for his life. Now he's holding his pants up with both hands and running as fast as he can. I can't help but break out laughing. All of a sudden the sky turns black with rocks. Rocks are bouncing off his head, his back, his legs, his arms; anywhere there's a spot to hit, he's being hit. I know it's a serious situation for him, but I can't help myself. I'm cracking up. I'm laughing so hard I'm crying. It's like a Three Stooges movie.

Finally he makes it back to his pick-up. "Day tries to keel me, Meester," he says. "Deed jew sees them, Meester; day tries to keel me?"

I'm gasping for air, but I manage to say, "Yes, I see them. That's why I don't go over there." He says, "Jew know what Meester, I hate dem Mexican sums a beeches. Day is all peenchy pendayhoe sums a beeches."

I'm a little shocked; after all he's a Mexican. He says, "I am marry Meester. My wife she ees Mexican." He points to his black eye and says, "Jew see thees Meester? My wife geev me these, Meester, an sheese a Mexican. Dats why I hate dem sums a beeches."

He asks me for a pen and a piece of paper, and then he writes his name and phone number down and gives it to me. He says, “Eef jew eber need hep agin Meester, call me, and I weel come hep jew. I really hates dem sums a beeches Meester."

With that he throws his red, white, and blue pick-up truck in reverse and tears out of there. I think he might have said as he rode out of sight, “Hi Yo, Seelver Away." Or was that my imagination. I've never seen him again, but I think of him often.

CHAPTER 15

The Mystery Load

At times it seems like I'm living on the West Railroad Bridge. This is one of those times. No matter how I work it, this bridge is not fun. To begin with though, it seemed like fun because there are so many people there that you can't help catching a bunch. It's like a cat and mouse game. It doesn't take very long for it to become work though.

Terry Pallaqi and I are working the bridge together today, so we're doing the job a little differently. We don't back off completely and try to catch them all. Instead we let a few of the more aggressive ones in, and catch them. The ones that remain on the bridge are a lot less trouble that way. We have been doing this for about six, nearly seven hours. It's getting old. We've caught, and processed approximately sixty aliens so far, and we still have at least two hours, and thirty minutes to go.

For the moment we were holding them back. I have just completed processing seven wets. Oops! Did I say "WETS."? Let me explain. Wets are a shortened version of "Wetbacks." In Mexico they are called "Mojados," which means the same thing. It's a descriptive term that's been derived from the fact that, people who cross the Rio Grande river by means of swimming or wading get wet, and when they are running away all you see is their backs, ergo "Wetbacks".

Although the majority are Mexican, a wetback can be from any country in the world, including the United States, and they can be a member of any race, including Anglo. Although most are laborers or become laborers because of their illegal status, it is not necessary to be a laborer to be a wetback. Anyone who crosses the river illegally, (and that has come to include anyone who crosses the border illegally) can and probably has been called a wetback.

Border Patrol agents routinely called illegal aliens wetbacks prior to the early 1980's. Then Political Correctness reared its head, and "wetback" was one of the first things to go. It has become a disciplinary matter if a Border Patrol agent is caught using the term "Wet," or "Wetback." It seems that some of the Hispanic organizations are personally offended by the term, feeling that it is both derogatory and aimed directly at them. I personally do not believe that to be the case, but I'm not here to argue that. It simply changes the way we identify the people we are arresting and processing. We have to come up with a different term. Illegal alien is the most generally accepted, but even that is controversial.

No matter what you call them, the majority of the people coming across the Rio Grande River illegally are Mexican. They are coming here strictly for economic reasons and have little desire to become United States citizens.

So here we are at the end of Chihuahua Street holding them back. Actually we're sitting in our vans shooting the breeze, telling each other lies, and, in the process, holding them back. Out of the corner of my eye, I notice a U-Haul truck pulling a compact pick-up truck followed by a sedan. As I watch, the truck and sedan pull around the corner behind us and park on the north side of the Allright Parking Lot. They don't park in the lot; they park on the street running along the north side of the lot. I'm thinking, 'if they want their vehicles to be watched, they should park inside the lot and not outside the lot. A man gets out of the U-Haul truck, and a woman gets out of the sedan. After walking around their vehicles a time or two, they walk over to the bridge and cross over into Juarez, Mexico.

We continue to hold back the people at the bridge. Nothing is happening. I guess the aliens have decided that it's hopeless. Even if they do get in, we will probably catch them.

About a half hour after that U-Haul truck parks over there on the street, I start to hear noises. It sounds like the noises are coming from inside the U-Haul van. I listen for a while, and then I tell Terry I'm going to go take a closer look.

When I approach the truck, I can hear several different sounds coming from inside. I try to identify the different sounds. One sound is very high pitched and sounds like a baby crying. Another sound is very low pitched and guttural. It sounds like a man grunting, a big man. Added to that is a pounding noise coming from all around the interior of the truck, and at times the truck is rocked back and forth, sometimes violently. I'm very puzzled.

I listen for a while, and then, after deciding that it has to be people, I try to talk to them. I knock on the side of the truck, and the noises stop. I try to find out who's in there. I shout, "Who's in there?" Nobody answers. So I shout it again, "Who's in there?" No answer. Now I'm really puzzled. Then the noises start up again. I knock on the side again, and the noises stop. I try one more time in Spanish. I shout, "Hola, quien esta?" ("Hello, who's in there?") No answer. I try again, but there's still no answer.

This is going to require a conference. I go back over to Terry and tell him what I've found. We talk about getting a bolt cutter and cutting the lock off but decide that really isn't our jurisdiction. If the lock is cut off, we decide it should be cut off by the City Police Department.

Terry decides to go over and take a look for himself. I stay and hold back the tide. I watch him walk around the truck and scratch his head. Then I watch and listen to him talk to the truck in English and then in Spanish, just like I had. Finally he comes back over and says, "I think we ought to call the P.D. and let them worry about it."

I say, "I think we should too." So we call the police.

The police show up about 15 minutes later. The police officer does the same thing we did: walks around the truck, knocks on the side of the truck and he talks to those in the truck in English and Spanish. Finally he calls his sergeant and asks him to come out to his location and to bring a bolt cutter with him.

The police sergeant arrives about 15 minutes later with the bolt cutters. He goes through the same routine again: Walks around the truck, knocks on the side, talks to whoever is in the truck in English and Spanish. Then we all look at each other and shake our heads. We all agree there is something fishy here, but nobody wants to cut that lock.

While we're considering all the possibilities, the owners show up. They want to know what's going on. We want to know what's going on also. The guy smiles at us and asks, “Do you want to look inside?"

“You’re damn right we want to look inside."

The guy gets his key out and opens the door. None of us are prepared for what we find inside. We're all dumb-founded.

The van contains a load of furniture, but along with the furniture is an orangutan, a Siamese cat, and a German Shepherd dog. The cat is roaming around free and yowling like Siamese cats do. Sounds just like a baby crying. The dog is also roaming free. Like German Shepherds do, he's walking the perimeter of the van, on top of all the furniture, and his wagging tail is banging the side of the van. It sounds just like someone pounding on the side of the van. The orangutan is in a cage. He's grunting and pulling on the bars of the cage, like orangutans do, causing the entire truck to rock. He really wants out of that cage. Every once in a while, he reaches outside the cage and bangs the side of the van with his big fist.

We all laugh. We were sure that truck was loaded with people. It's a big relief to find out it isn't.

The lady has just returned with an ice cream cone for the orangutan. She's insisting that he kiss her on the lips before she'll give him the cone. That's when we all decide to excuse ourselves and leave.

CHAPTER 16

Permanent Airport Duty

I've been working days at the airport for several weeks now, which in itself is not unusual, except for the day shift part. We normally work each activity for two months, but the shifts are rotated every two weeks. What is unusual is that if everything goes according to plan, I will be working days at the airport for as long as I want in the future. The reason for that is a new seniority system that the El Paso Sector is implementing on a trial basis.

Let me explain why management has decided to try this new system. First of all, morale has always been low at the El Paso Station. Recently though, morale has reached an all time low because of a liberal court decision which virtually ties our hands. This court decision states, in effect, that unless an agent personally observes a person crossing the border illegally or has personal knowledge of that person's illegal immigration status, the agent will not be allowed to stop and/or question that person as to his or her immigration status. This decision means that at least 75% of the arrests that we have been making in the past will not be allowed in the future.

The reason for this court decision stems from a raid that the Border Patrol made in conjunction with the Immigration Service and the El Paso Police Department. All Border Patrol Agents were ordered to participate in this raid, including pilots, intelligence agents, supervisors, The Patrol Agent in Charge, assistant chiefs, anti-smuggling agents, Border Patrol agents from out stations, etc. They were all utilized as Plain Clothes Border Patrol Agents, with the exception of the El Paso P.D.

The raid was aimed at the bars, topless bars, restaurants, and almost any establishment that serves the public in the El Paso area. The raid was successful. Over 700 illegal aliens were arrested, along with one United States citizen.

The one United States citizen was an El Paso fireman. The fireman was arrested by the El Paso P.D. for being drunk and disorderly. Of course, that is not how it was reported by the news media. When the reporters got hold of the story, it became a United States citizen falsely arrested by the United States Border Patrol as an illegal alien.

When it went to court, the liberal judge agreed with the media. He agreed because it gave him the opportunity to hand down a decision that he had been waiting to hand down for some time. This particular judge had felt for some time that the Border Patrol was out of control. Perhaps we had arrested his maid at one time or another. Who knows?

The raid was ill advised in the first place because of the feelings harbored by the judge. It never would have taken place if not for some extenuating circumstances. The Chief Patrol Agent in charge of the El Paso Sector for the past two years died suddenly and unexpectedly of a heart attack. A temporary Chief Patrol Agent has been detailed to El Paso from a different sector - a smaller, more rural sector. Almost every chief that has ever been detailed to one of the larger sectors, such as the El Paso Sector or the San Diego Sector, for whatever reason, feel like they have to make their mark. This Chief is no different he feels like he has to make his mark. That's what this raid is all about. It is an ego thing - a chief of a smaller sector watching how the El Paso Sector was being run and thinking, If I ever get a chance, I'll show them how to run that sector. He got his chance, and we had to pay.

We all fumbled around for a while, not knowing exactly what to do. The only people being caught, were caught right on the river. Management was beginning to complain about not enough apprehensions. Morale was about as low as it could go. We felt that management was not supporting us and that it was their fault that the numbers were down. That wasn't the only reason for the low morale. Mainly what we wanted was a chance to air our grievances and to have some voice in how we were treated in the future.

Then a strange thing happened. I've never seen it happen before or since. The word filtered around the station that there was going to be a work stoppage. Everyone would go to work, and everyone would be where he or she was supposed to be, but no one would apprehend anyone. The work stoppage would begin the following morning at 8:00 A.M., and would continue until management decided to talk to us. Now here's the strange part. Every agent in the El Paso Station cooperated. For the next three days, the Border Patrol caught not a single alien. Not one. There were a few, possibly three or four a day that were turned over to us from other agencies. That's it.

It took three days. The Patrol Agent in Charge did everything he knew how to do to get us back to work. What he knew how to do was intimidate. He patrolled the coffee shops and threatened anyone he caught there with disciplinary action. He is a big man, about six foot six inches and very intimidating. It didn't work. He didn't scare anyone. What he did succeed in doing was making a total ass of himself in front of several of the El Paso citizens.

The morning of the fourth day we had a station meeting. The Chief, Deputy Chief, Assistant Chiefs, and the Patrol Agent in Charge were all there. They listened; we talked. The most important thing to come out of that meeting was the seniority system.

The system works like this. Seniority is based on the amount of over all time an agent has in the Border Patrol. Agents are allowed to bid on the shift they desire and the activity they desire. The more desirable the activity or shift is, the more time in service is required to get it. For instance, the day shift requires the most amount of time in service of any of the three shifts and the mid-night shift the least amount of time. Of the activities, the Airport requires the most amount of time, and Line-watch the least amount of time.

I have nearly nine years in the patrol at this time, so I am able to get both the activity and the shift that I want. As a matter of fact, everyone on the day shift at the airport is considered an old timer. You can hear the whispers around the station, “There’s not going to be many apprehensions made on days at the airport”. Of course, there never had been much activity on days at the airport. We all assumed there just wasn’t much going on there during the day. Surprise, surprise! All of a sudden the day shift crew at the airport is arresting just as many people as any other shift. In addition to that, we're making as many smuggling cases as the rest of the station combined.

So that’s why I'm at the airport, and with any luck, I will never work the West Railroad Bridge again. I'm working with Freddy Flores and Davy Burton. Freddy is from Puerto Rico and can be rather obnoxious. This works out nicely when we were trying to break a smuggler by using the good guy, bad guy routine. Freddy can play the bad guy without even trying, which makes it easy for me to be the good guy. Davy, on the other hand, is more interested in taking care of personal business, which is what he's doing most of the time.

Freddy and I are standing at the bottom of the escalator watching people. I love it. I’m a people watcher by nature anyway. I really enjoy hanging out at the airport, watching people and the planes landing and taking off. I notice a lady about sixty five years old, and a young man around twenty eight or twenty nine years old walking toward the escalator. For some reason they catch my attention, even though I don’t think they are illegal aliens. About thirty or forty feet behind them walk three adults and a child. One of the adults appears to be illegal. I have a feeling they're all together, even though they are separated by a substantial distance and not attempting to make any contact with each other. Long ago I learned to rely on those feelings.

Those feelings or instincts are actually senses that have been developed by long periods of observation. Any law enforcement agent that is successful in his or her field has developed those senses. The agent is always looking for specific things that set the lawbreaker apart from the law-abiding citizen. These things vary according to what type of law the agent is enforcing.

For instance, a few of the things a Border Patrol Agent may look for are: types of clothing, where they were made, how they are being worn, whether they are new or have been worn before. Something else I watch for is: does the person appear to be looking for me or is he making an asserted effort to not be looking for me (the agent). Nervousness is another give away such as perspiring in an air-conditioned building. Another thing I look for is how the person walks. People, who spend their lives working in plowed ground, and/or having to walk as their only means of transportation, walk differently than most of us do. How they talk, what language they speak. How they act, are they familiar with things like escalators, doors that open automatically, etc? There are many other things that a Border Patrol Agent looks for, but this will give you an idea of what I mean.

When a person has looked for these things for months, or years, they become a part of his or her subconscious mind. They are recognizable at a glance. Many times the agent is unable to articulate how he knows that person is illegal; he just knows. But when the agent has to testify before a court of law he has to learn to articulate because hunches are not acceptable.

Freddy and I stop the first group, wait for the second group to catch up, and then we stop them also. We question all of them about their citizenship, and as I suspected, they all appear to be legal except the one adult in the second group. The old woman and the young man both have resident alien cards. I'm not completely sure about their cards, so we take them back with us to our office and put their cards under the black light to look for defects. At least that's the excuse that I use. I actually want to find out what their connection is to the young couple.

We share an office with the Immigration Inspectors on the first floor of the airport. It's located almost directly under the security checkpoint on the second floor. It's in the area where international passengers have to pass through to be inspected.

This area is where we take the two groups for further questioning. Because it is a fairly large area, we are able to keep everyone separated. We always try to keep the subjects separate, so that we can check one story against the other. Of course, they usually make up a story in advance and go over it several times to make sure everyone knows what to say. Even so, if enough pressure is applied, at least one or two will usually forget part of the story. If there is a child involved, you can almost always depend on them to tell the truth, at least what they know of the truth.

I start with the old woman and the young man. While I'm talking to the old lady, whose name is Leticia, I'm checking her resident alien card under the black light. We're standing at one of the stations that international passengers have to pass through to be inspected. The desk is one of those stand-up type desks, which you either stand near or sit on a high stool to use. I find out that it is attached solidly to the floor, and it's approximately two inches from the wall, which is also attached firmly to the floor. The way I find this out is that while questioning Leticia, who is very irate and being very obnoxious, I accidentally drop her card. The card scoots across the desk and drops into the space between the desk and the wall. I can't even see it until I get a flashlight. Then I can see it, but I can't reach it. After performing many contortions, I finally go looking for something to reach down between the wall and the desk. I find a broom, and then I borrow the gum that the younger woman is chewing and place it on the end of the broom. It takes a while, but eventually it works. I get the card back, and it's a good card.

While I'm retrieving the card, I continue questioning Leticia. All I manage to get out of her is that the young man with her is not her son, but is in fact, her boyfriend. She's sixty five, and he's twenty eight. She must have some qualities that I'm unable to see. Another thing that I discover is that neither one of them has an airline ticket.

By this time Freddy has managed to make everyone in the other group very angry. The young woman, whose name is Maria, is so pissed-off she refuses to speak at all. We decide to switch. Freddy will question Leticia and Victor (the boyfriend), and I will question the other group.

I start off with Paul, the young man. After talking with him for quite some time, I decide to take a chance. I say, "Your mother tells me that you're the smuggler and that she doesn't know anything about it."

He says, "That's not true; I'm not a smuggler. I didn't know that guy was a wetback."

Aha! She is his mother. I had suspected it, but then I thought the other guy was her son also.

Armed with this new information, I decide to question the daughter-in-law. Her name is Maria, and the little girl is Sara. Maria still isn't willing to say much, but she will talk to me. First off, she wants to tell me what an ass-hole Freddy is. I agree with her, and she likes that. Next she wants to tell me what a bitch her mother-in-law is. I agree again. Other than that, she isn't telling me anything. I try to talk to the little girl, Sara, but Maria keeps answering for her. It's beginning to look like I'm not going to get much more out of her than Freddy did.

I decide to try one more ploy. I tell her, "Well, it looks like I don't have any choice. I'm going to have to release your mother-in-law, and her boyfriend because I don't have anything on them. Would you like to send Sara home with Leticia?"

"Absolutely not," Maria says.

“OK, Do you have someone else that you can call to come and get Sara?"

“No. Why do I need someone to come and get Sara”?

“Because I’m going to have to confiscate your automobile, and put you and Paul in jail for alien smuggling." I don’t really believe that's going to happen, but there is a remote possibility that it could.

“No damn way am I going to jail for that bitch," she says.

It worked.

“She’s the smuggler. Paul and I just came along to the airport with her because she asked Paul, and he does everything she wants him to. We’ve never seen this guy before."

I decide to push it a little further I don’t know why, just one of those feelings. I say, “Sure, you say that now when you find out you’re going to jail. I would, too, but what proof do you have that this is true”?

“What do you mean proof?"

“I mean, what can you tell me that will prove to me that she’s smuggling the alien and not you."

“What if I tell you that there are more aliens and that they are in a house that she owns?"

"I think that might prove that she is the guilty one. Where is that house located?"

She tells me the address. Then she wants to tell me everything that her mother-in-law has ever done to her. I listen for quite a while, and then I excuse myself. I call the station and tell the agent on the desk to send a unit to the address she gave me and check it out. Tell them that if there are aliens there, just bring them to Sector Headquarters and we will be in to process them.

I tell Freddy what's going on, and he's incredulous. He can't believe Maria even talked to me, let alone told me where to find other aliens. Leticia is still denying everything. Freddy, by now is wishing he could beat a confession out of her. I say, "Forget it, Freddy; we don't need a confession from her now. We'll take her to the station, and if they bring in those other aliens, I think that will be enough. I think she will want to talk then to see if we won't go a little lighter on her."

When we get to the station, the other aliens are already there. There are eight of them, all males. When Leticia sees them, her complexion turns ashen. She immediately comes over to me and wants to talk. She still doesn't want to talk to Freddy, but she wants to talk to someone. She wants leniency. She says, "I'm an old woman. You can't put me in jail I will die. Well, I know you can put me in jail, but please don't, Mister. I won't ever do it again."

She's right, but she doesn't know it. I can't put her in jail. It's her first offense, and a judge will probably just turn her loose. I decide to let her squirm for a while though; maybe it will keep her from doing it again. She has a brand new four door Dodge sedan though, and it's paid for. We will seize that, of course.

After we finish processing all the aliens, I go over to talk to Leticia again. I say, “Leticia, we've decided not to put you in jail. We're going to seize your car instead. You will be given a hearing date, and at the hearing you will probably be allowed to pay a fine and get your car back”. She throws her arms around me and gives me a great big hug. She says, “Thank you, thank you, thank you." I'm looking over her shoulder at Freddy; he just shakes his head and walks away.

After they're released Freddy says, “Damn you Rambo, next time I’m going to be the good guy. You’re the son-of-a-bitch that took her car away from her, and I’m the one she hates."

I say, “Freddy, there ain’t no way you’re going to be the good guy; being an ass-hole is a way of life with you. It's more natural for you than it is for that old lady”.

CHAPTER 17

Going Somewhere

It's early March 1983; the weather in El Paso is lovely. Everyone is running around in their jeans and tee shirts. However the weather up north is not so nice. Denver just got a foot of snow.

We have a trainee working with us at the airport today. He, like Freddy, is from Puerto Rico. His name is Rudy Valdez, and I think he's going to be a pretty good agent. Rudy and I have been working up on the second floor around the gate areas. Actually Rudy has been doing most of the work, and I've been watching. It takes some watching to keep up with Rudy. He's young, full of piss and vinegar, and very enthusiastic about his job. Most of the trainees are very enthusiastic, at least until they get burned a few times by management. Then they slow down and become a bit more cautious. Rudy hasn't been burned yet.

I'm watching a situation unfold in front of me that reminds me of a situation that occurred when I was a trainee. I'm just waiting to see how Rudy handles it.

The situation I refer to occurred about eight or nine years ago. I'd been working with a journeyman named Joe Griffin. Some of the other trainees thought Joe was a difficult man to work with. Actually they thought he was an ass-hole. I didn't feel that way though. I think his dry sense of humor and his very stern manner probably confused some of the guys, but I understood him pretty well. I kind of liked him. Maybe it was the birds of a feather thing.

This situation occurred early in the morning, just as we were beginning our shift. We were about to go into the coffee shop to get a cup of coffee when we noticed a lady coming into the airport in her housecoat. She was a gringa (white woman) and had her hair in curlers. I thought she was probably coming to meet someone arriving on one of the flights. Then Joe pointed out a Hispanic lady that had walked into the airport about two minutes after the gringa lady. He said, “I think we ought to postpone the coffee for a few minutes and go check that lady out." I think he had the situation figured out already, but I didn’t.

We followed the Hispanic lady up to the gate. She appeared to be all by herself. She was carrying a small bag with her and was dressed for cooler weather. It was March, and the weather up north was much colder than it was in El Paso. Almost everywhere is up north from El Paso.

When she reached the security station, we were right behind her. She had some trouble figuring out exactly what they expected of her, for that reason Joe decided to question her before she went any further. She was already a little intimidated by the security guards and she admitted right off that she was here illegally.

Joe asked her for her ticket. We always took control of the ticket right away, because it prevented the aliens from running. Besides if we took the ticket back to the ticket agent, we could get it refunded for them. If they took it back themselves, the airline probably wouldn't refund it. If we had the ticket, and they ran, they never would get their money back. I'm sure Joe didn't think this lady was going to run, but I wasn't sure what he was thinking.

The lady didn't have a ticket. I wanted to search her purse and her bag to make sure she wasn't lying. Joe said, "She doesn't have a ticket what makes you think she does?"

I said, "Well, she's carrying a bag, and she's headed for the American Airlines gate."

Joe said, "So."

"So where in the hell does she think she's going without a ticket." I asked her that.

She said, "No se" (I don't know).

I asked her if she thought she could buy a ticket upstairs.

She said, "No se."

I gave up. Joe seemed to have it all figured out anyway.

I hadn't noticed till now, but we were still walking toward the gate. I said, "Where are we going."

He said, “We need to check the rest of the people."

“What people. The old gringa lady is the only one that has come up here so far."

“Let’s check her then."

He’s got to be kidding, I thought. She isn’t going anywhere. Not the way she’s dressed. He wasn’t kidding though. He walked right up to her, and said, “Hello ma’am, would you mind telling me where you’re from?"

She said, “Are you out of your mind? I’m a United States citizen, of course.”

“Of course, where are you going, Ma’am?"

“If it’s any of your business, I’m going to Chicago."

“Very well, Ma’am, may I see your ticket?" She was mad. She practically tore the zipper off her purse when she opened it. She jammed her hand down in the purse and came up with a ticket. I thought, Well I’ll be damned, she does have a ticket.

Joe said, “Ma’am, are you sure that ticket is for you and not for this young lady right here?"

She said, “Of course I’m sure, I don’t even know that person."

“Very well, Ma’am."

We went over and sat down by the wall. Of course, I knew what was going on now, but I didn't know what we could do about it. It was obvious that the white lady was smuggling the Mexican lady. The Mexican was probably a housekeeper, and she was probably being sent up to Chicago to work for some friend of the white woman. That's a lot of probably, and I couldn't see any way to prove it.

About ten minutes later the gringa started ambling back down the hall toward the airport lobby. We caught up with her before she had gone very far.

Joe said, "Where do you think your going ma'am?"

"Oh, I just thought I would go get a cup of coffee."

"Well, if you do, you are going to miss your flight. The plane is about to take off."

"Oh! It is"?

"Yes, Ma'am, it is, and I would suggest that you get on board the aircraft right now, so you don't miss it."

"Yes," she said. "I see what you mean." She didn't make any move to board the aircraft though.

Finally Joe said, "I don't think you understand, Ma'am. If you miss that plane, we are going to arrest you for attempting to smuggle this lady to Chicago".

You didn't have to be a psychic to know how she felt about Joe. There was fire in her eyes, and I thought I could see smoke curling up off the top of her head. She got on the plane though.

Going to Chicago in March in your housecoat, was certainly more punishment than she would have gotten if she had gone to the station with us.

I thought it was beautiful.

Now here I am with Rudy. He has three people sitting across the hall from me. There are two men and a woman. They appear to be illegal aliens. He has asked me to watch them for him while he talks to another couple. The other couple doesn't appear to be dressed to go anywhere. The man is wearing badly worn jeans and a tee shirt. The lady is wearing a thin summer dress. They have a little girl with them, and she's wearing rather soiled clothes. She is certainly not dressed for travel. I assume that Rudy has these people pegged as the smugglers of the three sitting against the wall.

Rudy is not happy though. In fact, he is very frustrated. He's bouncing back and forth between the two groups like a ping-pong ball. First he talks to the family; then he talks to the aliens; then he goes back to the family. This back and forth thing has been going on for about fifteen minutes.

The flight that's leaving from the gate that we're sitting in front of is a Southwest flight going to Denver. In fifteen minutes or less, the airplane will leave the gate.

Rudy has reached the end of his rope. He doesn't know what to do. He comes over and explains the situation to me.

He says, "I've got a problem here. Those people against the wall are all illegal, but they don't have any tickets. The guy that has the tickets is that guy over there with his wife and five year old child. He says the tickets are for them, but the flight is almost ready to leave, and they haven't boarded yet."

I say, "So what's the problem?"

"I want to arrest them, and take them to jail, but I can't prove anything - that's the problem."

I say, "In the first place, even if you could prove it, they probably wouldn't go to jail because of the child. In the second place, why put them in jail? Just make sure they get on that flight. You can probably do that by telling them that you will have to put them in jail if they don't get on that flight."

I'm looking directly at him, and it's as if I just turned the lights on. Thanks to Joe Griffin, Rudy thinks I'm a genius, and I'll never tell him any different.

The lady has been watching us. When Rudy tells them what he will do if they don't get on the airplane, she looks at me like she wants to kill me. Her husband starts to hustle though. He doesn't have any money, so he has to borrow money from the illegal aliens. They only have twenty dollars and that's what they give him. The woman takes the little girl over to the female alien for her to take care of her. When they start down the ramp to get on the airplane though, the little girl escapes and runs after her mother. They decide to take her with them.

I actually feel sorry for them. Here it is the end of February, and they're going to Denver, Colorado, dressed for 80-degree weather. The weather bureau is saying that it's snowing in Denver. They have a one-way ticket and only twenty dollars in their pockets. Oh, well! As the Mexicans say, “Mala suerte (bad luck)!”

Rudy tells everyone about it. "The best part," he says, "is no paper work."

CHAPTER 18

Villalobos

I have been up on the second floor where all the departure and arrival gates for the domestic flights are located. It has been a very slow day so I've been up here for quite some time just watching the planes take off and land. I'm watching for illegal aliens too, but I haven't been finding any. It's a pretty day without a cloud in the sky and I'm spending most of my time in the satellite. The satellite is a large round structure at the end of a long passage way. It's the Eastern-most portion of the airport, completely enclosed with windows, the view is fantastic.

As I sit here, I observe two Navy jet fighters on a short final approach to Runway 26L. The trailing aircraft is a very short distance behind the leading aircraft. They are landing in tandem, one right behind the other. I've watched these tandem landings several times, and I always wondered what the pilots would do if a problem occurred with the lead aircraft. On this day my question is answered.

As I watch, the lead aircraft touches down, and immediately the pilot ejects. The pilot and his seat are shot way up into the air, at least five or six hundred feet, maybe farther. The second aircraft is just about to touch down. The pilot has no choice. If he tries to go around, he might hit the other pilot, and if he stays with his aircraft, he will probably be unable to avoid the unmanned aircraft should it go out of control on the runway. He ejects.

Now we have two pilots dangling from their parachutes and floating gently to the ground while their jet planes streak down the runway. The lead aircraft swerves slowly to the right side of the runway. When the right main landing gear goes off the runway and hits the gravel, the aircraft makes a sliding right turn and comes to a stop about 50 feet from the runway. The only apparent damage to the aircraft is a blown-out tire on the right main landing gear, which blew-out on touch-down.

The other aircraft does not fare so well, however. It doesn't have a blown-out tire; in fact, there isn't anything wrong with this aircraft, except that it doesn't have a pilot. When it touches down, it's still set at approach power. It speeds the full length of the runway, off the end of the runway, through the cyclone fence that surrounds the El Paso International Airport, across Airport Road, through the cyclone fence that surrounds Fort Bliss, and it's headed straight for the guard shack that houses two military guards. By now it's dragging several yards of cyclone fence. Dragging the fence and plowing through the gravel slows the aircraft enough to allow the guard's time to escape from the guard shack. They're still running and looking back when the plane crashes into the shack and bursts into flames. It takes only a matter of minutes for the shack and the plane to burn completely to the ground.

A crew from Biggs Army Air Base, which adjoins El Paso International Airport to the north, comes over, puts a new tire on the remaining aircraft, and tows it away.

While members of the crew are towing the aircraft away, a call comes over the intercom for any available Border Patrol Agent to report to the Airport Security Office. I
start ambling toward the office. I'm at the far end of the airport, so I'm thinking there's probably another agent closer to the office that will respond to the call ahead of me. I'm wrong.

When I arrive, I find three young ladies sitting side-by-side on the bench against the wall talking to the security agent.

I ask the agent, "How can I help you?"

He says, "These young ladies have some questions for you concerning this lady's niece," and he points to the middle lady.

I say, "Go ahead. How can I help you?"

The lady introduces herself as Angelita and her two friends as Maria and Josefina. Angelita says, "I will tell you what happened. Maybe you can help us, or maybe not."

"Go ahead," I say.

"Last night about 8 o'clock I came to the airport with my niece. Her name is Veronica, and she is 16 years old. She is from Mexico, and she is going to Chicago. We went up the escalator and over to the x-ray machine. I was following behind her because she did not have a visa to go to Chicago and I did not want them (The Border Patrol) to think I was smuggling her. Veronica put her suitcase through the machine, and she started to walk through the other thing when the man showed her his badge."

"What did his badge look like," I ask?

She says, "It was a round, silver badge. He told her that he was a Border Patrol Agent, and he asked her where she was from, where she was going, and then he asked her for her Mica (Border Crossing Card). She didn't have one, so he said she would have to go with him. I don't think he was a Border Patrolman."

I didn't say anything, but at that point I didn't think he was a Border Patrol Agent either. The Border Patrol badge is not round and silver; it is shaped like a shield, and it is gold with a blue stripe across it. Furthermore, a Border Patrol Agent would have asked her for her resident alien card or her border crossing card and visa. Either of those would be good for travel to the interior of the United States. A border-crossing card without a visa is good for just that, crossing the border and remaining within 25 miles of the border.

"Why don't you think he was a Border Patrolman," I ask?

"Because, he just didn't look like a Border Patrolman," she said.

"How did he look?"

"He was a big man, and he had a pock marked face."

That sounds like Villalobos, I thought. "What was he wearing," I ask?

"He was wearing a brown sport jacket with a yellow shirt," she says.

"Did he say or do anything else that you can remember," I ask?

"Yes! He said he would take her to get her papers so she could go to Chicago."

"Where did he say he was going to take her to do that?"

"He didn't say where, but he said he would take her to see Tall Paul, and he could fix her papers for her."

Whoa! Very few people in the civilian world know anything about the Patrol Agent in Charge of the El Paso Station. He's six foot six inches tall, his name is Paul Henson, and everyone in the Border Patrol calls him Tall Paul. It's highly unlikely though that anyone other than a Border Patrol Agent would refer to him as Tall Paul. This is probably a Border Patrol Agent.

I ask the security agent, "May I use your phone, please?'

"Help your-self," he says.

I call station one and ask the agent at the desk, "How many females were arrested on the four to midnight shift at the airport last night?"

After a brief hesitation the answer comes back, "None."

"Were there any females named Veronica arrested at the airport yesterday?"

"Negative."

"Were there any females arrested at the airport yesterday?"

"Negative. There weren't any arrests at the airport yesterday."

"OK, thank you," I say and hang up.

I tell Angelita that nobody was arrested at the airport yesterday, not anyone for the entire day. She says, "Well, I didn't think it was a Border Patrolman."

I say, "I don't know if it's a Border Patrol Agent or not, but let me make another call."

I call Station One again and ask the agent at the desk, "Who worked the four to midnight shift at the airport last night?"

He checks the roster then says, "Capelo, Villalobos, and Resendez."

I say, "One more thing, who's working the four to midnight shift tonight?"

"Capelo, Villalobos, and Resendez."

"Thank you very much."

I tell Angelita, "The same three guys that worked the airport last night will be working here tonight. I suggest that you come back after 4:00 P.M. and talk to all three of them. If one of them is the same guy you saw last night, you should be able to get the truth."

She says she will and goes on to say, "My niece called me last night and said the guy that took her from the airport has gotten her a room at La Casa Blanca (The White House). She says he is being real nice, and he is going to be back in a little while and take her to see Tall Paul."

I say, "OK! I'm going to go over to the station and talk to the guys that worked here last night and tell them that you want to talk to them."

I leave the security station and go back to our airport office to do some research. I want to know where and what the White House is. I go through the white pages and yellow pages of the phone book looking for La Casa Blanca. I don't have any luck. Next I go through the white pages looking for The White House. Bingo! There it is - The White House Motel.

By this time it is about ten minutes to four so I go over to the Station to find Villalobos. I'm pretty well convinced that it was Villalobos that picked the girl up because of the description her aunt has given. I'm also convinced that if it was Villalobos, he's probably in big trouble. But if he hasn't done anything too criminal yet, he might be able to straighten things out.

When I arrive at Station One, the four to midnight shift is having roll call. I try to get Villalobo's attention to let him know that I want to talk to him after roll call, but I'm unable to. As soon as roll call is over, I go looking for him. It seems like he's trying to avoid me. I finally corner him in the executive rest-rooms (rest-rooms that are normally used by management).

After checking around and looking under all of the stalls to make sure there isn't anyone else listening to what I have to say, I say, "Rogelio this is what is happening at the airport today. I was summoned to the security office to talk to three young ladies. One of the ladies says that she was at the airport last night with her sixteen year-old niece and that a Border Patrol Agent detained her niece. The man she described matches your description. She says that her niece called her from The White House and told her that she is supposed to remain there until the agent takes her to see Tall Paul. She says Tall Paul is going to arrange her papers so she can go to Chicago. I checked with station one desk for apprehensions at the airport last night. The guy on the desk told me that there weren't any. Now, I don't know what went on at the airport last night and I don't want to know. I told those girls that I would talk to the crew that worked the airport last night and tell you to meet with them at the security office as soon as you could after 4:00 P.M. If things happened the way they appear to have happened, then I think you better get over there and explain to Angelita that her niece is safe and well, if she is. If it didn't happen that way, then you better explain that. No matter what happened, you better get your ass over there right now and talk to those girls. If you don't, they'll come back tomorrow to talk to me. Tomorrow I will advise them to file a missing person complaint with the El Paso Police, and, if asked I will tell the police everything that I have just told you."

Villalobos doesn't say a word throughout my entire conversation. When I finish talking, he says, "OK," and he walks out. How strange, I'm thinking. He acts like it has nothing to do with him.

I do my paper work and go home. I'm troubled for the rest of the night though because I'm not sure that I've done the right thing. Maybe I should have just told the lady to report her niece as a missing person, and not even given Villalobos a chance to do the right thing. Although, I'm not sure that Villalobos has even done anything at this point.

The next day when I go to the airport, I go straight to the security office. I ask the security guard if he knows anything about the lady that was in yesterday asking about her niece. He says he hasn't heard anything from her yet. I say, "OK, well, let me know if they if come in."

I leave the security office and go upstairs to check the gate areas. I don't hear anything from the aunt throughout the day, so I'm beginning to think that maybe Villalobos has taken my advice.

Then about 3:00 P.M. I get a call from security. I go to their office, and sure enough there sit the three ladies that I talked to the previous day. I've got a pretty good idea what I'm going to hear, but I asked the question anyway, "What happened last night?"

Angelita says, "Nothing, we waited here until seven o'clock last night, but no-one came around. Finally we went looking all over the airport, but we never did see anyone that looked like the man that took Veronica out of here."

I say, "I don't think you have any choice then. It looks like you're going to have to file a missing person report."

Angelita tells me, "I have already talked to the El Paso Police, and they're all ready to file the report. All they're waiting for now is for me to call and tell them to go ahead."

"You might as well make the call then," I say.

I've got a pretty good idea what's going to happen next. It hasn't taken me very long to figure out what's taken place, even though I don't have all the details. It won't take the police very long to figure things out either. I could be wrong, and I hope that I am, but if what I suspect is true, I want it out in the open as much as anyone. I've never had any time for a crooked lawman.

When the 4:00 P.M. to mid-night crew shows up, I'm waiting to talk to them. Villalobos is not working, but the other two are. I ask them, “What happened last night? Didn't Villalobos go talk to the girls in the security office?”

Capelo says, “What girls? I don't know about any girls.”

“Me neither,” Resendez says.

I start from the beginning and explain everything I know to them. They both look at each other; then they look at me. Capelo says, “That explains why he acted the way he did last night.”

“How did he act,” I say.

Capelo says, “He never worked the public area of the airport at all last night. He stayed in the office most of the night. He only left once and that was to check the bus terminal, at least that's what he said. Just before mid-night he left the office saying he was going to get off on time.”

Resendez says, “We thought he was acting kind of strange, but we didn't know anything about the girl.”

“I told the aunt to report it to the police,” I say.

"Good," says Capelo, "I would have reported it last night."

"Well, my thinking was, that if things hadn't gone too far already, it might all be taken care of very simply. I was hoping we could solve this without having to bring in another agency;"

It didn't take very long for the police to find the girl and determine who was responsible for taking her to the White House Motel, just as she had told her aunt. Not only was she easy to find, but also it was easy to determine how she got there. She was registered as Mrs. Villalobos, and the license number was registered to his personal vehicle.

Villalobos never returned to work at the airport. He spent some time working the desk before being given the choice of resigning or being fired. He chose to resign. He later went to trial and was convicted of abducting the girl from the airport. I think he was given a two year sentence and served about a year.

I heard later from a friend of his that his wife never knew the truth of why he was sent to jail. This friend said that she never did hear about the girl or the abduction or anything. It was hard to believe, but maybe she just didn't want to know.

CHAPTER 19

I'm Out of Here

For almost a year I have been planning my next move. It's not easy to get out of El Paso if you're not a member of the Texas Ring. The Texas Ring includes anyone from Texas and excludes anyone not from Texas. Almost everyone in upper management in El Paso is Texas Ring. They've managed so far to keep me here in El Paso and keep me at the GS-9 level. It may not be a conspiracy but it sure seems that way to me. I'm not the only one; it seems like anyone not a native of Texas has an uphill battle to get promoted here because of the Texas Ring. Maybe not everyone in the Border Patrol, but certainly everyone in the Border Patrol in Texas is aware of the Texas Ring. It is not an organization it's just a form of discrimination that is practiced against anyone not from Texas.

If an agent is not from Texas and puts in for a job that someone from Texas has put in for, the Texan will get the job. The other agent will either get a really bad evaluation or the person making the selection will be from Texas or something simple like that, but he will not get the job.

I have put in for several positions with the Border Patrol, as well as with other agencies, but have always been given such poor evaluations by my supervisors that I didn't have a chance of getting any of those jobs. The

Texas Ring has always been a source of irritation to me, but not a serious problem.

Now it is a problem because I want to get into the Pilot Training program. I know better than to draw attention to the training program, so I do exactly the opposite. Last year I put in an application for three Pilot Trainee positions. I didn't get any of them even though I had more time in the Patrol and more flying time than all but one other person on all of those lists.

When I found this out, I immediately sent a letter to The EEOC (Equal Employment Opportunity Commission) asking them for the criteria used to make the selection in each of these positions. The position locations were El Centro, California; Laredo, Texas; and Marfa, Texas. It took a while, but I finally got a reply. I was told the following in the return letter: The first two positions, El Centro and Laredo were not complete lists, (In other words, there were not seven names on either list) therefore the selections were made alphabetically. "ALPHABETICALLY" I was discriminated against because my name started with an "R". The third selection was made according to who had the highest score. This is how the system is <u>supposed</u> to work; a list of names is made up from the seven highest scores out of all the applicants. Once those names are given to the board, scores are no longer considered a factor; they are only used to determine the list. From then on the applicants are supposed to be evaluated on their qualifications for that particular position.

It looks as though the board did not follow procedure. I suppose I could fight it, and maybe I could win. But I know that EEO knows that I know, and for now that is good enough. I am pretty sure that next time will be different.

At this time I start my escape plan. I have been working my butt off at the airport for a couple of years and have not gotten any credit for it. I am aware that people have noticed though. For instance, Chief Henderson comes out to the airport at least once or twice a month to have lunch with me and whoever else happens to be working. He also comes back into the squad room several times a month and talks to me while I am writing up smuggling cases. I know that he knows I am writing a lot of smuggling cases. He probably doesn't know exactly how many I'm writing because nobody seems to know that. I decide that maybe it is high time that somebody does know, so I write my immediate supervisor Carlos Carrales a memo. In that memo I state that I think since he is getting credit for all these smuggling cases, that he should pass some of that credit on to where it really belongs, to the people that actually make the cases. I say I think he should try to get us a Unit Commendation, and that since Freddy and I have more smuggling cases between us than the rest of the station combined, which is true, maybe we deserve Outstanding Awards.

I continue to make several smuggling cases a week, and all in all just do my job. Then one day as I am writing up a smuggling case at Station One, Dog Dodson, one of the line supervisors and a 1st class ass kisser, comes in and throws a large manila envelope on top of my typewriter. I open it up and there is my Outstanding Award. Everyone I have ever known that received an Outstanding Award had it presented to them at an awards ceremony. Not me, however; mine gets thrown at me while I'm working a case. I guess that's what happens when you make supervisors out of coyote hunters and grader operators. That, and kiss ass is all Dog Dodson ever did with the Patrol. Every time I'm writing up a case out in the Station One squad room and the Chief comes back to see what's going on: here comes Dog out of the supervisor's office saying, "Hi, Chiefie. How's it going Chiefie." Yes, that's exactly what I heard and I find that behavior very sickening. I doubt if he ever worked six months as an agent prior to being promoted to supervisor, and it shows.

I've been hearing rumors about more pilot training positions being opened up. I've also just found an announcement for a position as Supervisory Patrol Agent in Whitefish, Montana. I would love to have either one of those jobs, but I know I will have to get an evaluation from my El Paso supervisors for that Whitefish job, and that will take me out of the running. Even though I have just been given an Outstanding Award, and have more smuggling cases than anyone in the El Paso Station, I know what that evaluation will look like. But I also know I can make it work for me. I'm going to use this Whitefish job as my smoke screen. These guys are assholes, but they're not intelligent assholes. I put in for the Supervisory job in Whitefish.

Like anything with the government it takes time, but eventually my Whitefish job application comes to the attention of my supervisor. I have a new supervisor now, his name is Jesse Delgado. All Jesse does is run his trap-lines (girls). He runs around all day with nothing more important to do than visit the girls at the airport, the bus terminal, the bridges, etc. All the while I'm making him look good with all those smuggling cases.

He pays me back with an evaluation that should have, and most certainly would have, gotten me fired if it were true. As soon as I get it I rush into the Patrol Agent in Charge's Office and throw it on his desk. I say, with all the indignation that I can muster, "Read that, and if you agree with it, I'm taking it to the Chief and see what he thinks of it. You are aware that I just received an Outstanding Award aren't you."

He says "there's no way you deserve this kind of an evaluation".

I knew the evaluation originated with him, but I guess he didn't think I knew.

I say, "I want out of his unit, and I want out today. There is no way I should have to work with someone that feels that way about me."

The PAIC says, "We'll see what we can do".

"No", I say, "You'll do it now, or I go to the Chief".

"All right you're out of there".

Just what I wanted. That would keep them thinking they had just screwed me out of the job I wanted.

In the mean-time I have put in for three more flying jobs, but this time I add a little twist. This time I put that letter to the EEOC right in with my applications.

Everything bumps along as usual, except that I try to keep my feud with Jesse Delgado going for effect.

Late in the evening I get a phone call at home. It's from one of my friends in the communications office. He says, "Congratulations, Rambo".

"For what", I say.

"Well I have a teletype here that says you are to report to McAllen, Texas, as there new pilot trainee".

"YeeeeHaw", I yell. "I want a copy of that put in my mail drawer".

"Can't do it", he says. "You're not supposed to know about it till the PAIC puts the teletype in your mail drawer or gives it to you personally. You'll have to wait till then. They could fire us both if they found out I told you".

"OK, I'll wait".

Well, I wait, and I wait. A week goes by, two weeks goes by - this is getting ridiculous. I call the radio operator up and asked him if they have picked up the teletype yet.

He says, "No." So I wait some more. Days go by and still no call.

Three weeks later a call comes for me at the airport. It's the EEO office. The girl says, "I'm just calling to ask if you still want a letter from us outlining the criteria used to make the selections for the pilot trainee positions".

"Sure I do."

I'm going to play this thing to the end. "Why wouldn't I?

"Well, I just thought since you have been selected for the McAllen position, you might not need them".

"You say I've been selected for the McAllen position".

"Yes", she said.

"Well, why wasn't I notified"?

"You were. A teletype was sent to the El Paso Sector Headquarters."

"Are you sure?"

"Yes, we have a receipt."

"Thank you very much. That's all I need. If I need you to send the criteria or the teletype, I will let you know."

I hang up the phone and head straight for Station One. I go straight to the PAIC's office and say, "Where's my teletype."

"What teletype," he says.

"The teletype that's in the radio room stating that I have been selected for the pilot training position in McAllen, Texas."

"I don't know about any teletype, and how would you know if there's one there?"

"You know damn well there's one there, and so does EEO. They're the ones that told me about it. They say it's been there for three weeks. That teletype better magically appear in my mailbox within the next five minutes, or I'm going to call them back".

I go to the coke machine and get myself a coke, and then go to my mail drawer, and there it is.

I'm outta here. Next stop McAllen, Texas.

I know the only reason I am able to get out of El Paso is that I am lucky and had a few tricks up my sleeve. There is one other reason though, and that reason is my good friend the Chief Patrol Agent in McAllen, Texas. He just happens to be from El Paso, and we knew each other before he became Chief in McAllen. If he hadn't selected me, I'd have probably retired as a GS-9 in El Paso, Texas.

On the other hand, if I had not gotten a notification from EEO, that teletype could have set in there forever, and it would not have been the first time. It has happened many times in government service when someone has been selected and simply not been notified. When that happens it's a double whammy, because the people who have made the selection get rather angry when the person selected does not show up, and many times the person gets black-listed and will never be selected again.

Our tax dollars at work.

Printed in the United States
135807LV00004B/1/P